JOURNAL

OF THE

ROYAL ASIATIC SOCIETY

China in Shanghai

Journal
OF THE
Royal Asiatic Society

China in Shanghai

New Series, Vol. 74, No. 1, 2010

EDITORS
Lindsay Shen, PhD. and Janet M. Roberts

Copyright 2010 RAS China in Shanghai.

The Journal of the Royal Asiatic Society China in Shanghai is published by Earnshaw Books on behalf of the Royal Asiatic Society China in Shanghai.

CONTRIBUTIONS
The editors of the Journal invite submission of original unpublished scholarly articles and book reviews on the religion and philosophy, art and architecture, archaeology, anthropology and environment, of China. Books sent for review will be donated to the Royal Asiatic Society China in Shanghai Library. Contributors receive a copy of the Journal.

SUBSCRIPTIONS
Members receive a copy of the journal, with their paid annual membership fee. Individual copies will be sold to non-members, as available.

LIBRARY POLICY
Copies and back issues of the Journal are available in the library. The library is available to members.

www.royalasiaticsociety.org.cn

Journal of the Royal Asiatic Society China in Shanghai
Vol. 74, No. 1 (April 2010)

ISBN-13: 978-988-19091-0-7

EB085

© 2010 China Economic Review Publishing (HK)

China Economic Review Publishing (HK) Limited for Earnshaw Books
1804, 18/F New Victory House,
93-103 Wing Lok Street, Sheung Wan, Hong Kong

All rights reserved. No part of this book may be reproduced in material form, by any means, whether graphic, electronic, mechanical or other, including photocopying or information storage, in whole or in part. May not be used to prepare other publications without written permission from the publisher.

CONTENTS

	Page
Preface	1
A Letter from the Editors	2
Humans Must Conquer Nature:Philosophical and Religious Sources of China's Environmental Ideology	
By James Miller	4
Unanswered Questions: Notes On The Life Of Arthur de Carle Sowerby	
By Peter Hibbard	22
Florence Ayscough in Shanghai: Interpreting China through Autobiography	
By Lindsay Shen	32
Amy Lowell: The Fragrance of Adapted ChineseVerse in *Fir Flower Tablets*	
By Janet Roberts	64
The Clark Family and Weihai	
By Zhang Jianguo and Zhang Junyong	100
Japanese People in Modern Shanghai	
By Chen Zu'en	
Translated by Catherine Dongyuan Yin	112
British Clubs and Associations in Old Shanghai	
By Nenad Djordjevic	123
'Memento Glory': Yang Jing in the context of her time and beyond	
By Emily de Wolfe Pettit	140

Susan Sontag's 'Project for a Trip to China'
    By Janet Roberts   146

POETRY

Plane Trees, Spring and Fall (Hefei Nanlu)
    By Andrea Lingenfelter   149

Shanghai Poems
    By Thomas McCarthy   150

A Lute from Tung Tree Wood
    By Janet Roberts   152

BOOK REVIEWS

Them and Us and Them: The Catalpa Series
    By Paul French   153

Stairway to Heaven: A Journey to the Summit
of Mount Emei by James Hargett
    By Friederike Assandri   160

British Rule in China: Law and Justice in
Weihaiwei, 1898-1930, by Carol G S Tan
    By Liu Wei   163

China Cuckoo by Mark Kitto
    By Tess Johnston   167

White Salt Mountain:
Words in Time by Peter Sanger
    By Lindsay Shen   169

The Man Who Loved China
by Simon Winchester
    By Kim Taylor   170

The Jacquinot Safe Zone, Wartime Refugees in
Shanghai by Marcia R. Ristaino.
    By Li Tiangang   175

Peking Sun, Shanghai Moon: a China Memoir by Diana
Hutchins
Angulo
    By Janet Roberts   177

Missy's China: Letters from Hangzhou 1934-1937
by Doris Arnold
    By Lindsay Shen   179

A Study of the North China Branch of the Royal
Asiatic Society by Wang Yi.
    By Liu Wei and Judith Kolbas   182

CONTRIBUTORS   185

x

PREFACE

After a hiatus of over 60 years, we are proud to re-launch the Journal of the Royal Asiatic Society China in Shanghai. In 1858 the Society, then called the North-China Branch of the Royal Asiatic Society, launched its prestigious journal. Until its last issue in 1948, the journal was internationally recognized for its authority, and richly contributed to the understanding of Chinese culture in the English language. It was, and still is, widely cited in scholarship on China. Its contributors included many eminent sinologists such as Alexander Wylie, Herbert A. Giles, Reginald F. Johnston, James Legge, John C. Ferguson and Emil Bretschneider.

The Journal's articles explored Chinese history, culture and landscape with a heady mix of scholarly confidence, imagination and curiosity. Subjects ranged bravely: 'the Mutton Wine of the Mongols'; 'Sailing Directions from Woosung to Hankow'; 'Chinese Names for Boats and Boat gear'; 'Alligators in China'; 'How Snow Inspired Verse'; 'China's Petrified Sun Rays': 'Cosmical phenomena observed in the neighborhood of Shanghai, during the past thirteen centuries'. Their authors speculated ('What did the ancient Chinese know of the Greeks and Romans?'); they tirelessly documented and catalogued; they debated, argued and rejoined.

In a similar spirit, this new chapter of the Journal's existence will, we trust, be shaped by restless curiosity and innovative scholarship. In this first issue we pay tribute to the Society's history through articles on two dedicated former RAS members and prolific journal contributors, Arthur de Carle Sowerby and Florence Ayscough. This issue explores aspects of Shanghai's past, but also presents poetry on its present. It looks backwards at issues such as Colonialism, but also examines such currently vital subjects as China's environmental ideology. It is the ambition of the Society that its journal should once again be a repository of outstanding scholarship on historic and contemporary China.

PETER HIBBARD MBE (President) and Editors

A LETTER FROM THE EDITORS

Dear Readers,
It has been our distinct pleasure, as honorary editors, to compile and edit this inaugural Journal of the Royal Asiatic Society China in Shanghai. We have chosen, as the theme, for this revitalized journal, a thread to the past and a perspective on the present, in China.

In this issue, our president Peter Hibbard and Dr. Lindsay Shen explore the lives of two important RAS figures from the early part of the 20th century - Arthur de Carle Sowerby, a former president, and Florence Ayscough, a former librarian of the North China Branch of the Royal Asiatic Society. In the articles by the honorary co-editors, Lindsay Shen and Janet Roberts, is found their collaborative research on the creation of *The Fir Flower Tablets*, by Ayscough and her childhood friend, the Pulitzer prize winning New England poet, Amy Lowell, who set out to translate classical poetry into Chinese and then adapt the poems into English.

To further extend this dialogue about translation of Chinese poetry and English poems inspired by China, we included contemporary poetry about Shanghai by the acclaimed contemporary Irish poet, Thomas McCarthy. We include two poems by Dr. Andrea Lingenfelter who is currently translating the works of Chengdu and Shanghai poets. An "adapted" poem by Janet Roberts is a solo postscript, along with Peter Sanger's *White Salt Mountain: Words in Time,* which is reviewed by Lindsay Shen, as an answer to her own quest for a biography to be written about Florence Asycough.

Janet Roberts also contributes a short essay on relatively unknown associations between Susan Sontag and China. Emily de Wolfe Pettit, a resident of Beijing and London offers an insightful appraisal of a contemporary artist, to underscore the vital developments in the international art arena.

To highlight the current green campaign, in China, Dr. James Miller's article on Ecology and Taoism, was chosen, as a result of invitations sent by the editors, in late 2008, to all presenters in our RAS lecture series. Other past speakers whose works are found in this volume include Nenad Djordjevic, an honorary vice president of the RAS China in Shanghai, on clubs and associations in old Shanghai, Zhang Jianguo on the British history in Weihai and Professor Chen Zu'en on the Japanese in Shanghai.

In our Book Reviews, we hoped to achieve a balance, in keeping with our theme of the old and new, of classical academic issues, and of contemporary concerns. Dr. Kim Taylor, the Society's Honorary Librarian, and a former fellow at the Needham Institute, appropriately reviews Simon Winchester's book, *The Man Who Loved China,* a biography of Joseph Needham. Dr. Judith Kolbas, who refounded the RAS in Hangzhou, and Dr. Liu Wei, another honorary vice president, review a history of the North China Branch of the Royal Asiatic Society. Tess Johnston, local historical chronicler, has reviewed Mark Kitto's *China Cuckoo* and the co-editors have reviewed Tess Johnston's two edited memoirs of women living in China in early 20th century. Paul French, prolific author and the Society's Director of Research and Publications, offers his insights, in the review of the current Catalpa series, edited by Lynn Pan, from HK/Yale University Press, which includes her own book *Shanghai Style* and a book by British Museum librarian, Francis Wood, *The Lure of China.* Professor Li Tiangang of Fudan University reviews Dr. Marcia Ristaino's, *The Jacquinot Safe Zone,* while Dr. Assandri critically appraises a book on the sacred mount Emei by one of our past lecturers, Professor James Hargett.

We hope you will find as much pleasure in reading the author's carefully researched articles on past and present China. We are grateful to all our contributors in this rebirth of the Journal of the Royal Asiatic Society China in Shanghai.

JANET ROBERTS
LINDSAY SHEN, *PhD.*
Editors

HUMANS MUST CONQUER NATURE

Philosophical and Religious Sources of China's Environmental Ideology

JAMES MILLER

ABSTRACT

Traditional Chinese philosophy is well known for its monistic cosmology in which heaven, earth, and human beings are mutually implicated in an evolving organic process known as the Way (*dao*). This vision is broadly shared by Daoists and Confucians and was the cosmological foundation of the state ideology of Imperial China. Tu Weiming refers to this as an "anthropocosmic" vision, which he contrasts with Cartesian dualism, instrumental rationality and the entire logical underpinnings of the Western Enlightenment mentality. This logic, according to standard interpretations of Chinese modernization, was adopted into, by the May 4th generation of Chinese modernizers in the early 20th century. The implication of this view is that the ills associated with modernization, including, in particular, the alienation of human subjectivity from objective nature, derive from the Western Enlightenment mentality and are not endemic, within Chinese culture. This paper argues, however, that the history of Chinese concepts of nature has not been uniform or monolithic, and there exists within traditional Chinese culture, philosophy and religion a wide range of views about the relationship between human beings and their natural environment. In particular, the paper draws attention to the history of more dualistic paradigms in which nature and human beings are viewed as being pitted together in a struggle for supremacy. The conclusion to be drawn from this is that the origin of China's contemporary environmental woes cannot be located simply in the rejection of traditional Chinese culture and the adoption of Western enlightenment values. In fact Mao's glorification of the human struggle with nature has deep roots within Chinese culture and history.

INTRODUCTION

In 2000, the American Academy of Arts and Science published an issue of its journal *Daedalus* on the topic of modernity considered from a variety of cultural perspectives. In that issue, the contemporary Confucian scholar Tu Weiming made the following argument regarding the Chinese encounter with modernity in the twentieth century (2000: 201):

> The modern West's dichotomous world view (spirit/matter, mind/body, physical/mental, sacred/profane, creator/creature, God/man, subject/object) is diametrically opposed to the Chinese holistic mode of thinking. Arguably, it is also a significant departure from ancient Greek, Judaic, and early Christian spiritual traditions. Informed by Bacon's knowledge as power and Darwin's survival through competitiveness, the Enlightenment mentality is so radically different from any style of thought familiar to the Chinese mind that it challenges all dimensions of the Sinic world. While the Enlightenment faith in instrumental rationality fueled by the Faustian drive to explore, know and subdue nature spurred spectacular progress in science and technology, it also became a justification for imperialist domination and colonial exploitation. As the international rules of the game, defined in terms of wealth and power, were superimposed on China by gunboat diplomacy, Chinese intellectuals accepted the inevitability of Westernization as a a necessary strategy for survival.

Here, Tu Weiming is proposing a narrative by means of which to explain the revolutionary changes that China experienced in the twentieth century: China's intellectuals abandoned their holistic mode of thinking in which heaven, earth and humanity were considered parts of a mutually interdependent evolving cosmos, and instead adopted a dichotomous Western mode of thinking in which humanity is placed in opposition to nature. This choice was forced upon China by the colonial aggressions of the West in the nineteenth century, and was adopted as a "necessary strategy" rather than by free choice or desire.

The consequences of this way of thinking about China's encounter with modernity are twofold: firstly, China's encounter with modernity is to be understood fully and solely within the context of China's violent and humiliating engagement with the West in the nineteenth century; secondly, therefore, the negative consequences associated with modernization are also the product of this violent encounter and are not intrinsic elements of traditional Chinese ways of thinking. In other words, the process of modernization undertaken by China's revolutionaries in the twentieth century was a strategic choice to embrace Western thinking and did not emerge in an organic way from China's cultural traditions. The question that this paper attempts to answer is the extent to which the negative environmental consequences associated with modernization were also the product of this violent encounter and subsequent "strategic choice" and, conversely, the extent to which they were supported by traditional Chinese culture. The reason for asking this question is that if the negative consequences of modernization can be blamed fully on the process of Westernization, then there is hope for thinking that the rehabilitation of Chinese tradition that is currently under way in the People's Republic of China may also yield patterns of thought and habits of action that are beneficial for China's transition to an ecologically sustainable future. If, on the other hand, the negative environmental consequence of modernization were abetted in China by elements of traditional Chinese culture, then the current revival of interest in traditional Chinese culture may not necessarily be as beneficial for the environment as authors such as Tu Weiming imply.

MODERNIZATION

Of all the various consequences of modernization, the one under consideration here is the Weberian concept of *Entzauberung*, variously translated as disenchantment or rationalization. The basis for this concept is that the modern world is to be distinguished from the pre-modern world by its embrace of rationality not simply as a philosophical principle but also as a practical strategy for engaging the world:

> The modern world is organized in a rational way. This means that clearly specified goals are pursued by a calculated allocation of means; the means include not only tools but also human activity and men themselves. These things are treated instrumentally and not as ends in themselves. Effectiveness and evidence are kings. The procedures are also rational in the sense of being orderly and rule-bound: like cases are treated alike. (Gellner 1987: 153)

The consequences of this modern process of rationalization are to be felt not simply in the way nation states are organized, based on the rule of law, but also, more broadly, in terms of the view of nature that this implies:

> It is not only the procedures of organizations which are, in this sense, 'bureaucratised'; the same also happens to our vision of nature, of the external world. Its comprehensibility and manipulability are purchased by means of subsuming its events under orderly, symmetrical, precisely articulated generalisations and explanatory models. This is Disenchantment: the Faustian purchase of cognitive, technological and administrative power, by the surrender of our previous meaningful, humanly suffused, humanly responsive, if often, also menacing or capricious world. That is abandoned in favour of a more predictable, more amenable, but coldly indifferent and uncosy world." (Gellner 1987: 153)

Here Gellner, interpreting Weber, agrees with Tu Weiming on the centrality of this Faustian bargain driven by moderns: through science, we gain knowledge over the natural world, and thus, the power to reshape it through technology (Tu's instrumental rationality); but this comes at the expense of a loss of intimacy or a feeling of interdependence with the natural world. (The

Romantic movement in the West can thus be understood as an attempt to regain the feeling of intimacy with nature that was lost in this transformation). Tu's argument that China's intellectuals adopted a strategy of revolution in the 20th century can also be viewed as an extension of this Faustian bargain: Chinese modernizers made a strategic, rational calculation to adopt alien patterns of thinking and social forms in order to gain mastery of their own destiny and reshape China as a strong and independent power. Abandoned in this process is what Tu terms "the Chinese holistic mode of thinking." The implication is that were China to embrace once again its "holistic mode of thinking" then this would go some way towards mitigating the negative effects associated with modernization.

As a logical argument, this makes perfect sense. The question here is to what extent China's traditional culture and philosophy can correctly be categorized as a "holistic mode of thinking." Might it not be overstating the case to suggest that this way of thought was dominant within Chinese philosophy and culture?

Holistic Thought and its Impact

The basic source for holistic thinking in Chinese philosophy is what Tu Weiming terms Confucianism's "anthropocosmic vision" and can be divided into two main principles. The first is the concept of resonance (ganying); the second is the Neo-Confucian concept of a monistic cosmos patterned from vital force (Qi). The concepts of vital force and resonance rise to the fore in philosophical and medical literature of the former Han dynasty. Robert Weller (2006: 24) cites one such text in which resonance is understood as a cosmic force that joins disparate elements together:

> When the magnet seeks iron, something pulls it, when trees planted close together [lean] apart, something pushes them. When the sage faces south and stands with a mind bent on loving and benefiting the people, and before his orders have been issued, the [people of the world] all crane their necks and stand on tip-toe; it is because he has

communicated with the people via the Vital Essence.

By the time of the Neo-Confucian philosophers of the Song dynasty (960-1279) these intuitions of invisible cosmic forces had been worked into a monistic cosmology based on the concept of *Qi* or vital force, especially as elaborated by the philosophy Zhang Zai (1020-1077) in his famous Western Inscription. It begins thus:

> Heaven is my father and Earth is my mother, and even such a small creature as I find an intimate place in their midst. Therefore that which fills the universe I regard as my body and that which directs the universe I consider as my nature. All people are my brothers and sisters, and all things are my companions. (Trans. Chan 1963: 497).

That which "fills the universe" is *Qi*, the universal cosmic power. Tu Weiming cites Zhang Zai's explanation of *Qi* as follows:

> [*Qi*] fills the universe. And as it completely provides for the flourish[ing] and transformation of all things, it is all the more spatially unrestricted. As it is not spatially restricted, it operates in time and proceeds with time. From morning to evening, from spring to summer, and from the present tracing back to the past, there is no time at which it does not operate, and there is no time at which it does not produce. Consequently, as one sprout bursts forth it becomes a tree with a thousand big branches, and as one egg evolves, it progressively becomes a fish capable of swallowing a ship. (Quoted in Tu 1998: 112)

Tu's term for this dominant Neo-Confucian view of *Qi* is "the continuity of being" a phrase that denotes a holistic, integrated cosmos in which no element of being is absolutely separated from any other element. This is precisely the view that he opposes to the Enlightenment mentality which focuses on radical dualisms between spirit and matter and self and other, as opposed to the complementary Chinese dualisms of heaven and earth, or *yin* and *yang*. In the Confucian view, therefore, heaven and humanity ideally form a harmonious unity (*tian ren he yi*). The Japanese Confucian Okada Takehiko understands this view as implying an ethical matrix that unites the human world with the non-human. In an interview with Rodney Taylor, he reports:

> Yes I think we do [have this responsibility], and such an ideal should be extended to all forms of life, animals and plants alike. The Confucian concept of being in community (forming one body) with other human beings can be extended to the community of life itself. ... All humankind has a mind that cannot bear to see the suffering of others and this is something that should be applied to all life. (Taylor 1998: 47)

There is much evidence to suggest, however, that this ideal view of the unity of the cosmos failed to translate historically into harmonious human relationships with nature. Historians of the Chinese environment suggest that Chinese people have been in an aggressively adversarial relationship with their environment for millennia. Richard von Glahn's (1987) study of the expansion of the Han empire into present-day Sichuan (south-west China) involved the transformation of the native people's "civilization of the forest" by the Han Chinese "civilization of the plains." The result was the emergence of a revitalized economy based on the commercial exploitation of non-renewable natural resources such as minerals and timber from the frontier regions by the wealthy urban elite. The economic pattern of Han Chinese colonial expansion thus bears important similarities with the colonial expansion into the Americas and even the present-day resource economy of Canada.

More problematic still is the conclusion to Mark Elvin's (2004) massive environmental history of China, *The Retreat of the Elephants*:

> The religious, philosophical, literary, and historical texts

surveyed and translated in the foregoing pages have been rich sources of description, insight, and even, perhaps, inspiration. But the dominant ideas and ideologies, which were often to some degree in contradiction with each other, appear to have little explanatory power in determining why what seems actually to have happened to the Chinese environment happened the way it did. Occasionally, yes, Buddhism helped to safeguard trees around monasteries. The law-enforced mystique shrouding Qing imperial tombs kept their surroundings untouched by more than minimal economic exploitation. but in general, no. There seems no case for thinking that, some details apart, the Chinese anthropogenic environment was developed and maintained in the way it was over the long run of more than three millennia because of particular characteristically Chinese beliefs or perceptions. or, at least, not in comparison with the massive effects of the pursuit of power and profit in the arena provided by the possibilities and limitations of the Chinese natural world, and the technologies that grew from interactions with them. (Elvin 2004: 470-471).

In other words, as regards the anthropogenic effects of three millennia of Chinese civilization upon the natural environment, Chinese beliefs and perceptions were of relatively little consequence in comparison to the "massive effects of the pursuit of power and profit." This view, however, discounts the notion that the "pursuit of power and profit" is itself a cultural perception. Moreover, it assumes that the Neo-Confucian view of a harmonious unity between humans and their environments, in fact, represented the dominant cultural perception.

The argument I wish to pursue in the remaining part of this essay is that the Neo-Confucian ideal represented simply that: an ideal perpetuated by a tradition of elite academics that represented not the dominant cultural perception of nature but rather the ideal view that nurtured centuries of Confucian scholarship and was strategically denigrated by China's modernizers.

Humans must Conquer Nature

The radical alternative to the idealistic Confucian view of human-nature relationships is to be found in the four-character phrase "Humans Must Conquer Nature" (*ren ding sheng tian*) a slogan that gained popularity in the Maoist period and which is commonly associated with the environmental devastation that China's revolutionaries brought about in the twentieth century. This concept is most clearly elucidated in Shapiro (2001) which provides a wealth of evidence to argue that specific elements of Maoist ideology rather than simple ignorance or stupidity were responsible for the massive environmental problems that began to plague China in the twentieth century. In particular, Shapiro identifies political repression, utopian urgency, and dogmatic formalism as three key components of Maoist ideology, each playing an important role in exacerbating environmental problems or in hindering attempts to mitigate them. Altogether, these factors constituted what Shapiro terms a "war on nature," a war that was conceptually predicated in Mao's philosophy of voluntarism in which ideas were viewed as "having the power to mobilize efforts to transform the material world" (Shapiro 2001: 67). Willpower would compensate for China's lack of technological development, and ideas would "unleash raw labor to conquer and remold nature." Shapiro continues:

> "Man must conquer nature" [*Ren Ding Sheng Tian*], Mao declared, sounding the phrase that many Chinese mention as the core of Mao's attitude towards the natural world. (67)

The impression Shapiro gives here is that Mao's "declaration of war" on nature constituted a new development in the history of China's relationship with its environment, or at the very least, a new development in the conception of nature that was promulgated among the people. In fact, the four character phrase "Man must conquer nature" has a long historical pedigree that is worth investigating more carefully in order to assess the extent to which Mao's voluntarism represented a revolutionary and wholly novel concept of the environment, or whether Mao was activating a strand of Chinese thinking about the environment that has deep historical roots.

The key to understanding this four-character slogan is the word "nature" (*tian*). The root meaning of this word is "sky" or "heaven" and refers not to the earthly domain of living creatures but more mysteriously to the heavenly forces that in traditional Chinese cosmology were thought to direct human fate. To struggle against and conquer *tian* is thus to assert the primacy of the human spirit over and against the cosmic powers that define the various parameters of human existence including most especially the time of one's birth and death, and whether one's life will be blessed by good fortune, prosperity and happiness. In this context, therefore, the concept of heaven or sky (*tian*) is closely related to the concept of fate or destiny (*ming*) and, indeed, the two terms are most famously connected in the binome "mandate of heaven" (*tianming*) referring to the authority to rule bestowed on emperors by the heavens. The concept of "conquering nature," (*sheng tian*), therefore, does not necessarily imply any kind of environmental consequence in the sense of the human relationship with the natural environment. It can equally take on a more existential or even spiritual aspect, referring to human life as a constant struggle against the vicissitudes of fate.

This aspect of the "struggle with nature" can be illuminated by considering Chinese religion and popular culture. In the context of popular Chinese religion, temples are filled each day with people inquiring as to the auspicious days for marriage, conducting business affairs, or winning in the casino. All this network of religious activity presupposes a concept of fate or "given-ness," the pre-ordained limits within which individual lives operate, and against which individual lives struggle. Popular religion can thus be understood as pleading with gods to alter one's fate, or learning through divination what one's fate is to be. In both these cases, one can view popular sacred spaces as arenas in which the negotiation with fate or "struggle against nature" takes place.

In contrast to the popular religious tradition of negotiating one's destiny with the heavenly gods, the leitmotiv of China's longevity traditions is the opposite: "my destiny is my own and does not lie with the heavens" (*wo ming zai wo bu zai tian*). Proponents of Chinese longevity (*yangsheng*) techniques thus argued that the necessities for prolonging life were within the reach of the individual body and could be attained through various energetic (*qi*) practices and did not necessarily require the intervention of divine beings or heavenly forces (see Robinet 2000: 212). Longevity practitioners thus operated from the same framework as religious practitioners; that is to say, the concept of life as a struggle against the fore-ordained limits of existence, but the arena for negotiating with fate was not considered to be the local temple, but rather one's own body.

To take a further example, we can examine the arena of Chinese popular culture, in which the concept of struggling with fate continues to hold meaning. The four character phrase *ren ding sheng tian* appears, for example, in the title of a 2003 Hong Kong comedy with the English title Fate Fighter (Cheng Wai-Man 2003). The film tells the story of an ill-fated young man who struggles to obtain the good-fortune with which heaven has endowed his brother. This again serves as an example that the phrase "conquering nature" does not necessarily imply the negative environmental consequences associated with Maoism. Rather, it can have a more existential connotation, as these three examples indicate.

This is not to say, however, that the anti-environmental connotations of "struggling with nature" were produced as a result of Maoist voluntarism. Indeed this essay seeks to make the contrary argument, that the idea of struggling against nature is deep-rooted within Chinese thought and culture and was not invented ex nihilo by China's revolutionaries in the 20th century.

The connection here is that the concept of *tian* as "heaven" or "destiny" also covers some of the same semantic range as in the English "environment" and "nature." To struggle against one's fate is, especially in a pre-modern society, to struggle against the limits that nature and environment place on the ability to fulfill one's potential. Indeed, the historical context of a nation struggling against all manner of natural disasters such as flooding and famine makes the idealistic Confucian vision of harmony with nature all the more remarkable. The semantic overlap of biological nature and heavenly destiny is revealed most clearly in the Chinese myth "Jingwei fills the seas" (Jingwei *tian hai*), a classic tale from the Scripture of Mountains and Seas (*Shan hai jing*; 3rd century B.C.E). The myth tells of the daughter of the sun god Yandi who drowned in the eastern sea. In death, she was transformed into Jingwei, a bird who forever after, carried little branches and dropped them into the sea in a futile attempt to fill it up. The phrase "Jingwei tian hai" is now an idiom meaning "determination in the face of great odds," and can be interpreted either positively as a story of the indomitable human spirit, or negatively, somewhat similar to the English phrase "banging one's head against a brick wall."

Whether one chooses to interpret this myth positively or negatively, one thing is clear: In this story, Jingwei's struggle is both against fate and the physical environment. The natural environment, in the form of the sea, provides the context in which Jingwei's struggle takes on its meaning. Jingwei's struggle to fill up the sea with branches thus symbolizes the eternal struggle of human beings against their fate. In this story, therefore, nature, fate and environment are bound together to form the overarching context for human existence. This is hardly surprising in a country that historically, and into the present, has been defined by its struggles against floods.

The relationship between heaven and humans is thus that heaven commands or mandates the circumstances in which humans exist. Heaven defines the contours of people's lives, in the same way that in astrology, the position of the stars and the planets creates the basic disposition for individual human lives. Heaven demarcates the finitude of human existence and at the same time poses an existential challenge to human beings to overcome the limitations or conditions of existence that have been imposed upon them. These limitations or conditions of existence, especially in pre-modern China, may be concretely experienced by human beings in their struggles against the power of nature, especially as revealed in floods and other natural disasters, such as earthquakes.

NATURE AS A DISCRETE DOMAIN OF COSMIC POWER
The examples above reveal a concept of humans and their environment (whether interpreted physically or existentially) in an antagonistic relationship with each other. An alternative strand of interpretation also exists within the Chinese tradition, which views heaven/nature to be fundamentally distinct from the realm of human beings and not related to them in a necessarily antagonistic way.

The biography of Wu Zisu (d. c. 484 B.C.E.) recorded by Sima Qian (145-90 B.C.E.) records the phrase "I have heard that human masses defeat nature, and nature indeed also destroys humans." This idea seems to indicate a complementary rather than adversarial relationship between humans and nature. In effect, humans and nature operate in separate domains of power, and that although nature does indeed destroy human beings, it is also the case that humans destroy nature. The implication is that it would be a mistake to attribute agency to the part of nature, to imagine that the natural world has a deliberate bent against human beings. Rather, the fact that nature destroys humans and vice versa simply indicates the natural function of their separate purposes.

This view was articulated most fully by the Confucian philosopher Xunzi (313-230 B.C.E.):

When the stars fall or the sacred trees groan, all the people become afraid and ask: "What is the significance of all this?" I would say: "There is no special significance. This is just due to a modification of Heaven [or nature] and earth and the mutation of the yin and yang. These are rare phenomena. We may marvel at them but we should not fear them." (trans. de Bary 1960: 102)

This view stands in contrast to the more organismic view that saw heavenly portents and natural disasters as signs of some dysfunction in the realm of human affairs. In such a view, religious sacrifices or other rituals might play a role in readjusting the cosmic equilibrium between the state and the heavens in the same way that a doctor might administer acupuncture to readjust the flow of qi inside a patient's body. Xunzi, on the other hand, refused to believe that humans have the ability to influence nature on a cosmic scale, and had a more sophisticated view of the function of religious rituals.

If people pray for rain and it rains, how is that? I would say: Nothing in particular. Just as when people do not pray for rain it also rains. When people try to save the sun or moon from being swallowed up [in eclipse], or when they pray for rain in a drought, or when they decide an important affair only after divination—this is not because they think in this way they will get what they seek, but only to add a touch of ritual to it. Hence the gentleman takes it as a matter of ritual, whereas the common man thinks it is supernatural. He who takes it as a matter of ritual will suffer no harm; he who thinks it is supernatural will suffer harm. ... (de Bary 1960: 103)

Xunzi's view of ritual—and therefore religion—is not as an economic mediator between human desires and heavenly supplies, constantly adjusting the tension between the two. Indeed, he clearly denounces popular religious prayers to gods as form of idle superstition. Ritual is useful because it performs valuable psychological and communal functions, not because it actually produces some magical manipulation of nature. This is because in Xunzi's view, heaven, that is, the disposition of affairs in nature, is quite simply beyond human control.

This view of discrete domains reached its apogee in the work of the Tang dynasty literatus Liu Yuxi (772-842) in an essay "On Nature" (Lun tian) in which he wrote:

The power of nature is [the power to do what] humans in fact cannot do; the power of humans is [the power to do what] nature also cannot do. Thus I say "Nature and humans mutually defeat each other."

According to Luo Jianjin (1999), Liu Yuxi "pointed out that nature and humans each have their own capacities and incapacities. Here 'defeat' means 'be superior to', 'exceed', 'be stronger than,' and does not mean 'vanquish in battle.' The above text is a comparison of the respective strengths of nature and humans." In this interpretation, therefore, the concept of humans "defeating" nature and vice versa does not indicate some cosmic war or eternal struggle between humans and the heavens or the natural world, but rather that each operates in its own domain.

NATURE AS OBSTACLE TO PROGRESS
Having reviewed these various connotations of the phrase "humans must defeat nature" it is clear that the phrase does not necessarily connote the anti-environmental ideology that Shapiro seems to suggest. It is also clear that this phrase was not invented in the Maoist period but has a deeper history within Chinese culture. Shapiro is right, however, to locate the Maoist interpretation of the phrase by reference to Mao's voluntarist philosophy. In this philosophical outlook, the word "nature" is simply a cipher for whatever Mao deemed to be an obstacle to revolution. A famous statement of Mao Zedong in his youth was "To struggle with heaven [or nature] is fun forever! To struggle with earth is fun forever! To struggle with people is fun forever!" In these statements "Heaven" or "nature" connotes all manner of insurmountable social problems and cannot be simply equated with a biological context for human life. For example, when Mao famously cited the story of the Foolish Old Man who Moved the Mountain (Yu gong yi shan) from the Daoist philosopher Liezi (c. 4th century B.C.E), he interpreted the mountain as the "three mountains of oppression", namely, feudalism, bureaucratic capitalism, and imperialism (Liu 1999). Here we can see

Mao distinctively brought the concept of "defeating nature" into the social realm.

Despite the Maoist instinct to view all manner of problems through a political lens, the historical overlap in meaning between heaven, nature and fate persisted into the twentieth century. The Maoist struggle for revolutionary transformation thus bound together the natural environment, religious superstition (as the mediation between humans and fate), and social oppression as enemies of human progress. By the mid-twentieth century, therefore, "humans must defeat nature" became a popular slogan that signified the human spirit locked in a struggle to overcome social, environmental, and theological enemies. At the beginning of her book, Shapiro (2001: vii) quotes a famous revolutionary song: "Let's attack here! / Drive away the mountain gods / Break down the stone walls / To bring out those 200 million tons of coal." Here coal-mining is revealed as a theological, economic and political activity: it is a theological activity because it destroys the habitats of the local gods who were thought to reside in the mountain; it is an economic activity because the coal enables economic progress; and it is a political activity because it locates China's revolutionary progress in the hands of its workers and not its elites. Shapiro is right, nonetheless, to attribute the environmental disasters of 20th century China to Maoist ideology, but the phrase "war against nature" needs to be understood in a more nuanced way. Tian or "nature" was not always to be taken literally as denoting the biological context for human life. It also connoted the heavens—and even the gods themselves—as counter-revolutionary agents; and it could also connote any social force that was deemed an obstacle to progress. In this regard, Mao was not inventing something new but drawing on a rich heritage of Chinese cultural thinking about the relationship between human beings and their existential contexts.

From this perspective, China's modernization cannot simply be viewed as the overthrow of traditional understandings of nature, as the Weberian concept of disenchantment implies. In the Chinese context, the secularization of nature implicit in the phrase "driving away the mountain gods" was also bound up with thoroughly traditional Chinese understandings of nature as an obstacle to the human spirit, and was not simply a modern invention. Furthermore, the Maoist use of nature or heaven (*tian*) as a cipher for any obstacle to human progress indicates a continuing role for the theological view of life as cosmic struggle between humans and their divinely-mandated fate. Mao's use of this term as a site of "utopian urgency", in fact, goes against the secular strain of Chinese thought in which humans and the natural world were viewed as discrete and unrelated domains of existence.

List of Works Cited

Cheng Wai-Man. 2003. *Dou hap ji yan ding sing tin* 赌侠之人定胜天 (A Conman Conquers Nature). Hong Kong.

de Bary, Theodore Wm. 1960. *Sources of Chinese Tradition*. New York: Columbia University Press.

Elvin, Mark 2004. *The Retreat of the Elephants: An Environmental History of China*. New Haven: Yale University Press

Gellner, Ernest. 1987. *Culture, Identity and Politics*. Cambridge: Cambridge University Press

Glahn, Richard von. 1988. *The Country of Streams and Grottoes: Expansion, Settlement, and the Civilizing of the Sichuan Frontier in Song Times*. Harvard East Asian Monographs. Cambridge: Harvard University Asia Center.

Luo Jianjin. 1999. "Reflection on the history of the concept "humans must defeat heaven" *Dui ren ding sheng tian de lishi fansi*. Chinese Library Code 1000-0763(2001)05-0068-06

Robinet, Isabelle. 2000. "Shangqing—Highest Clarity" in *Daoism Handbook* edited by Livia Kohn. Leiden: Brill.

Shapiro, Judith. 2001. *Mao's War Against Nature: Politics and the Environment in Revolutionary China*. Cambridge: Cambridge University Press.

Tu Weiming. 1998. "The Continuity of Being: Chinese Visions of Nature." Pp. 105-121 in *Confucianism and Ecology* edited by Mary Evelyn Tucker and John Berthrong. Cambridge, MA. Harvard University Press.

_____. 2000. "Implications of the Rise of 'Confucian' East Asia," *Dædalus* 129.1 (Winter 2000): 201

Weller, Robert. 2006. *Discovering Nature: Globalization and Environmental Culture in China and Taiwan.* Cambridge: Cambridge University Press.

UNANSWERED QUESTIONS
Notes On The Life Of Arthur de Carle Sowerby
PETER HIBBARD

As far as I am aware, there are two published sources that document the remarkable life of Arthur de Carle Sowerby. One, in the form of a short book, comes from the pen of R. R. Sowerby[1] who describes himself as a 'distant kinsman' and the other comes from an article by Keith Stevens.[2] Apart from personal letters, R. R. Sowerby draws upon Arthur de Carle Sowerby's own compilation of his family history in *The Sowerby Saga*, of which three unpublished volumes were completed in 1952. Apart from summarising Sowerby's life in China, highlighting in particular his involvement with the North China Branch of the Royal Asiatic Society (NCBRAS), this short essay will attempt to shed some light on what Stevens refers to as 'unanswered questions.' One question was about the fate of *The Sowerby Saga* as 'nothing more is known about his work.' Fortunately, with more material in the public domain now, the author has located a copy of this work, together with some correspondence and personal diaries, which answer some, yet pose many more questions about the life of Arthur de Carle Sowerby.[3]

Sowerby was of distinguished stock and his adeptness in both the arts and sciences was born of family tradition. His great-great-grandfather, James Sowerby was a famous botanist and the author of the thirty-six volume *English Botany*. His eldest son, born to the daughter of a French Huguenot family of artists, James de Carle Sowerby, was one of the founders of the Royal Botanical Society. Sowerby's close relatives also included Anthony Stewart, famous miniature painter and William Seguier, founder and first curator of the National Gallery in London. His father, Reverend Arthur Sowerby, came to China in 1882 to help establish a Baptist Mission in the city of Taiyuan, the capital of Shanxi province. Arthur de Carle Sowerby, one of six offspring, was born there on July 8, 1855. Fortunately the family was on leave in England at the time of the Boxer Rebellion in 1900 when many fellow missionaries and around 8,000 Christian converts were murdered in the city. Sowerby was enrolled at the Bath Art and Technical School and then studied sciences at Bristol University. However he did not complete his Bachelor of Science degree, choosing to abscond to Canada following a failed love affair. Sowerby rejoined his family in China in 1905. R. R. Sowerby recounts that he returned equipped with 'rifle and hunting-knife, with the vague prospect of hunting and exploring in the unknown mountains of Northern China.'

Sowerby's dream became a reality just a year later when he took part in the Duke of Bedford's Exploration of Eastern Asia to collect specimens for the British Museum. Shortly afterwards Sowerby struck up a relationship, which was to last a lifetime, with New York tycoon Robert Sterling Clark. He accompanied Clark on his 1908-1909 expedition to Shanxi, Shaanxi and Gansu provinces to collect specimens for the United States National Museum in Washington. Such expeditions for the museum, funded by Clark, continued over the years 1910 to 1917 and from 1921 to 1931. Sowerby's travels took him to the wilder and less known parts of the northern and eastern provinces, as well as the Ordos Desert, Inner Mongolia, Manchuria and North Korea, and resulted in a large series of books covering with his travels, shooting adventures and the wildlife, flora and fauna of the regions.

The severity of life in the wilds took a toll on Sowerby's health and he was first stricken with arthritis whilst hunting in Jilin province in late 1914. The affliction thwarted his ambition to fight in France during World War I, though he was posted, to his disgust, at the headquarters of the Chinese Labour Corps on the Somme. Whilst in Paris Sowerby had the chance to renew his acquaintance with Clark, then a major in the US Army, and to plan new expeditions in southern China. He also had the opportunity to make a new acquaintance, albeit indirectly, with 'Dimples,' a friend of his brother Ted. Sowerby was requested to write to her by Ted who had been temporally blinded in France during the war. Some three

decades on 'Dimples' became Sowerby's third wife.

Sowerby settled in England immediately after the war to write his five-volume opus *The Naturalist in Manchuria*. He travelled back to China and Shanghai, via Washington in 1921, eager to set off for an expedition in Yunnan province. However yet again Sowerby was disappointed as Clark annulled the funding for the venture on account of the region being overrun with bandits. That, together with an ever-increasing frequency of arthritic attacks, curtailed further participation in major expeditions for 36-year old Sowerby.

Sowerby wasted little time in establishing himself and making his interests and ambitions known to the public upon settling in Shanghai in 1922. He established and assumed the presidency of The China Society of Science and Arts, an institution with kindred ambitions to those of the North China Branch of the Royal Asiatic Society, desirous of 'bringing about a better understanding and sympathy with the Chinese people on the part of the people of other nations.'[4] The Society was best know for its periodical *The China Journal of Science and Arts*, later simply known as *The China Journal*, which Sowerby founded with the editorial assistance of Dr. John C. Ferguson, adviser on educational affairs to the Chinese Government, and American born Ms. Clarice Sara Moise as assistant editor and manager.

The journal's first bi-monthly issue appeared in January 1923. Sowerby's belief that it was 'the best thing of its kind that has ever been produced in the Far East'[5] was validated when it became a monthly publication in 1925. The journal, which Sowerby edited from its inception until 1937, tells us much about the man and his interests with articles on topics from politics, natural history and art, Chinese history and Chinese industries, to hunting, shooting and fishing. The Society also organised monthly lectures.

Sowerby and his Society, however, had far greater ambitions beyond those of the printed and spoken word, and even beyond those of the NCBRAS. He wished for Shanghai to have a Science and Arts Museum, of greater scope and splendour than that of the RAS Shanghai Museum, which he once described as a 'stuffed bird show.' The two societies began some form of convergence in 1922 when Sowerby assumed the post of honorary curator of the RAS Shanghai Museum, jointly with Dr. Noel Davis. Sowerby had initially joined the NCBRAS in 1916 and published an article on *Recent Research upon the Mammalia of North China* in its journal that year and another on *The Natural History of China* in 1922. Sowerby, in his role as president of The China Society of Arts and Science, continued to lobby hard for their own new museum. However his request for financial support from the Shanghai Municipal Council (SMC) in 1923 was bluntly turned down. By the time that the subject again came to public attention in early 1926, the Society had already staged two art exhibitions and Sowerby made a plea to the SMC to raise a small levy on rates to support such a public institution. Perhaps his dependency on his personal benefactor, Robert Sterling Clark, coloured his view that the general public should not be called on to raise funds. He wryly surmised that the burden would fall on a few generous benefactors, whilst the majority of the Shanghai would reap the benefit for free.[6] His pleas again fell on deaf ears.

When Sowerby became the sole honorary curator of the RAS Shanghai Museum in 1927 his attentions turned towards creating a new museum for the RAS. Its collection had far outgrown the confines of the small and outdated building it had occupied part of since 1874. Sowerby began 'to agitate for its demolition and the erection of a new one.' Matters reached a critical point in 1930 when the old building was condemned and demolished. Sowerby again made passionate pleas to the SMC for funding. Initially these were ignored and in response Sowerby wrote 'considering the size and importance of Shanghai, the Municipal Council ought to be ashamed of itself that there is not a Municipal Building containing all these things (a museum, library, reading room, art gallery and lecture hall). It is an eternal disgrace to this city that the men who have served her all these years have failed to realize the intellectual needs of her residents and to do anything but maintain a town band, at enormous expense, towards meeting those needs.'[7] Eventually the Council agreed to pay around half the cost of the new building, leaving the public to find the rest. In an effort to raise civic awareness Sowerby established the British Residents' Association in 1931, vowing to involve more his kind with the running of Shanghai's International Concession. Described as 'a champion of the rights of the average citizen'[8] Sowerby made a failed attempt to become an SMC councillor in March 1932.

Shortly after, Sowerby was made Honorary Director of the Museum and given the welcome authority to proceed with its installation in the new RAS building. The China Society of Science and Arts was incorporated into the NCBRAS in 1933 and RAS Shanghai Museum was opened in November that year. In a rare reference to the RAS in his 1949 diary he tells of the museum that 'I practically created and which certainly would never have been there at all in its present form but for me.' It was the third institution of its kind in China with which he had been connected. The first was a small museum in Taiyuan, for which he provided most of the natural history specimens in 1905, and the second the Anglo-Chinese College Museum in Tientsin (Tianjin) in 1907.

As the limited confines of the new RAS building wouldn't allow space for an art gallery, Sowerby continued to plead for its cause: 'who ever heard of a city (except Shanghai) with a population running into millions not having an art gallery for the exhibition of modern or contemporary paintings?' he asked.[9] He was one voice, amongst many, who called for the conversion of the former Majestic Hotel into a genuine civic centre. However such a scheme was regarded as too extravagant and Shanghai remained bereft of an art gallery.[10] Sowerby took on further responsibilities when he initiated and assumed presidency of the Numismatic Society of China in 1934 and he was elected President of the NCBRAS in 1935, an esteemed office that he held until late 1940.

Under his presidency Sowerby had some success in transforming the RAS into a cultural institution. On the business side Mr. and Mrs. Sowerby sold most of their interest in *The China Journal* in early 1938, though his articles continued to appear in the publication up until August 1941.

The Mrs. Sowerby in question was Arthur de Carle Sowerby's second wife, Clarice Sara (née Moise), assistant and later manager of *The China Journal*. Stevens and R. R. Sowerby have conflicting accounts of their union in Shanghai with the former asserting that they were married in 1922 (even though in the 'Post Post Script' provided by Carl Smith it appears as 1925), whereas Sowerby asserts that they married in 1925 and set up *The China Journal* then. Sowerby's date is actually correct, but he seems to have confused the establishment with the advent of a monthly edition of the journal in 1925, largely due to the business acumen and marketing skills of Mrs. Sowerby. Clarice had in fact put in half the money required to start the journal in 1923, with the other half coming from her husband to be. The confusion stems from one of Stevens' unanswered questions - what became of Sowerby's first wife? He notes that Sowerby was first married 'around 1910' and that by the time he arrived in Shanghai this had been 'quietly forgotten.' R. R. Sowerby devotes just one sentence in his book to the matter: 'Shortly after this (Clark) expedition ended, Arthur de Carle Sowerby married Miss Mary Anne Mesny, daughter of the late John Mesny of Guernsey Channel Islands, and there is one son of the marriage living in Australia.'

Sowerby did in fact marry Miss Mesny, who was born of a Chinese mother, in October 1909 and from his letters it is evident that they were like-minded and enjoyed a very close relationship. May, as she is referred to, use to accompany Arthur on his expeditions before their son, Arthur Mesny de Carle Sowerby, was born in 1910 whilst they were living in England. They returned to China in the following year. The full story of how they came to be parted remains to be uncovered, but it is evident that the first Mrs. Sowerby had intent to divorce her husband before 1922 and remained in London on his second return to China in 1921. Following the finalisation of the divorce, Sowerby married Clarice in December 1925. The couple lived in comfort in a beautiful house, littered with a fine collection of Chinese pottery and porcelain, on fashionable Lucerne Road.

Life for the Sowerbys was turned head over heels when the Japanese Navy destroyed everything in the *The China Journal* offices following the Japanese occupation of the International Settlement on December 8, 1941. Both were initially exempted from internment, on account of ill health. However, following Clarice's death in 1944 Sowerby spent six months at what he described as the 'Lincoln Avenue Concentration Camp,' before being transferred to the Shanghai General Hospital for the last eight months of the war. Following the war he spent a few months back at his old house, whilst his last ten months in China were fittingly spent at his apartment above the RAS Shanghai Museum. He remained director of the museum until his departure from Shanghai, with his new wife Alice Muriel (née Cowens), bound for England aboard the *President Polk* on September 15, 1946.

Leaving China was a traumatic experience for Sowerby who, entertaining thoughts of death, described his life as at a 'dead end.' However by May 1947 his mental and physical faculties had recovered sufficiently for him to undertake a motor tour of England before heading off for America, arriving in New York on August 17. The Sowerbys eventually settled in Washington in July 1949 following troublesome dealings in getting some form of legal residency for Mr. Sowerby. His later years were filled with great anxiety and recurrent health problems.

Another of Stevens' unanswered questions refers to Sowerby's financial affairs. As Sowerby himself noted in a letter to Clark of October 25, 1924 'I have not tried to make money all these years - I have placed science first and foremost. And here I am with no prospects, down to my last penny.' Financial insecurity plagued Sowerby till his dying days. It appears that he had been financially supporting his first wife up until 1949, when his finances became so poor that he could no longer afford to do so. He was still in touch with his son at that point, though it appears unlikely that much support came from him as he was 'having a hard time in Buenos Aires.' However 'Sonny,' as his father refers to him, was able to offer financial assistance a few years later when living in London. Whilst it is beyond the realm of these notes to go further into his financial affairs, it is fair to surmise that Clark's support for Sowerby and his ventures went well beyond the funding of his work for the National Museum in Washington.

An examination of *The Sowerby Saga* and Sowerby's 1949 diary poses many more questions about the whereabouts of other manuscripts that may have been penned during the last five years of his life. Sowerby recounts that he kept an 'intimate diary' from February 1941 to his departure from Shanghai, though this does not appear among the holdings at the Smithsonian Institution. Furthermore I have been unable to find any trace of *The World Odyssey of a Naturalist,* recounting his experiences since leaving Shanghai, for which he was looking for a publisher in 1949. Presumably he was unsuccessful, or it may have never been finished. However the biggest mystery of all relates to the existence and whereabouts of further parts of *The Sowerby Saga*. Frustratingly, Sowerby gives little away about his personal life in the three parts of this work. The large group of family and friends who had inspected the first two parts of his manuscript also felt such frustration, urging Sowerby to divulge more about his personal life in the future. In his preface to part three of the work dated June 5, 1952 Sowerby vows to include more of his own autobiography in part four, with the assurance that 'further parts will be prepared and issued as necessity or expediency demand.' R. R. Sowerby, one of the relatives who examined the manuscript, reveals that three further parts were planned.

Thanks to the disclosure of a series of reports[11] from a private detective agency hired by Robert Sterling Clark to monitor Sowerby's finances and activities in 1950, there is evidence that Sowerby was working on some 'sort of biography of his life and experiences' in the later part of 1952. However Sowerby's efforts to continue his research and writing were increasingly hampered by ill health, largely confining him to the walls of his apartment at the Fairfax Hotel in Washington. The final report from the agency, dated November 9, 1953 notes that the book is 'not half finished,' and that 'the subject's physical appearance caused me to wonder whether (it) will ever be finished.' Arthur de Carle Sowerby died on August 16, 1954 and whether he managed to enlarge or finish his manuscript remains one of the unanswered questions that the author will be investigating and hopefully reporting on in next year's edition of this journal.

Why Worry?

I wonder why folks worry. There are only two reasons for worry: either you are successful or you are not successful. If you are successful there is nothing to worry about. If you are not successful there are only two things to worry about: your health is either good or you are sick. If you health is good there is nothing to worry about. If you are sick there are only two things to worry about. You are either going to get well or you are going to die. If you are going to die there are only two things to worry about. You are either going to Heaven or you are not going to Heaven: and if you are going to Heaven there is nothing to worry about. If you are going to the other place you will be so busy shaking hands with your old friends that you will not have time to worry ...... so, why worry?

Undated ditty from Arthur de Carle Sowerby

Endnotes

1 R. R. Sowerby: *Sowerby of China*, Titus Wilson and Son, Ltd., Kendal, 1956.
2 Keith Stevens: *Naturalist, Author, Artist, Explorer And Editor And An Almost Forgotten President*, Journal of the Hong Kong Branch of the Royal Asiatic Society, Vol. 38, 1998.
This article can be downloaded from: http://sunzi1.lib.hku.hk/hkjo/article.jsp?book=44&issue=440040
3 *Arthur de Carle Sowerby Papers, 1904-1954 and undated*, Record Unit 7263, Smithsonian Institution Archives, Washington DC.
4 *North-China Herald* January 16, 1926.
5 Letter from Sowerby to Clark dated January 22, 1922.
6 *North-China Herald*, January 16, 1926.
7 *The Municipal Council and the R.A.S. Building*, The China Journal, Vol. XII June, 1930 No. 6.
8 *The China Press*, March 17, 1932.
9 *North-China Herald*, April 19, 1933, p. 83.
10 Ironically the former RAS Building in Shanghai opened as a commercial art gallery in 2010.
11 The Clark. http://maca.cdmhost.com

PostScript: Since completing this article the author has been made aware of the existence, but unable to secure a copy, of a short book by Arthur de Carle Sowerby, *The Saga of an Invisible Friendship*, published in the year following his death.

FLORENCE AYSCOUGH IN SHANGHAI

Interpreting China through Autobiography

LINDSAY SHEN

A DIFFERENT MAP OF SHANGHAI

Each map of Shanghai tells a different truth: there are those that show the radiating waves of urban development, or the drawing and redrawing of political boundaries, the web of waterways, the location of toilets and the wharf for night soil transport, the tides of land values, the pockmarked progress of contagious disease, or the city as charted by the children of migrant workers.[1] Most maps are public, but some are purely private—short-hand diagrams, for instance, scrawled on envelopes, showing the location of a restaurant or the route between two homes. One private map that became public appeared as the endpapers to a posthumous book of correspondence between the American poet Amy Lowell (1874-1925) and Florence Ayscough (1875-1942), a writer and sinologist who spent much of her life in Shanghai, and a prominent member of the North China Branch of the Royal Asiatic Society (NCBRAS) *figure 1*.[2]

This map is a line drawing by one of Ayscough's friends, American artist Mrs. Alfred Dunlap, showing the route from the Bund to "Mecca"—Ayscough's Chinese-style home she named The Grass Hut by Yellow Reach, at 72 Penang Road.[3] Confidently idiosyncratic, it spotlights certain landmarks, while ignoring others; a notable omission along the Bund, for instance, is that bastion of British male privilege, the Shanghai Club. Instead, the American Woman's Club, the Country Club, and the Foreign YMCA appear prominently on Bubbling Well Road, just west of the soaring department stores Sincere and Wing On. And, possibly surprisingly for a city decried as crassly commercial, this map privileges the cultural, picturing buildings such as the Shanghai Art Club, the Alliance Française, the city's major theatres, the Chinese Library, and the Royal Asiatic Society on Museum Road.

Mapping is not simply a mensural but also a political,

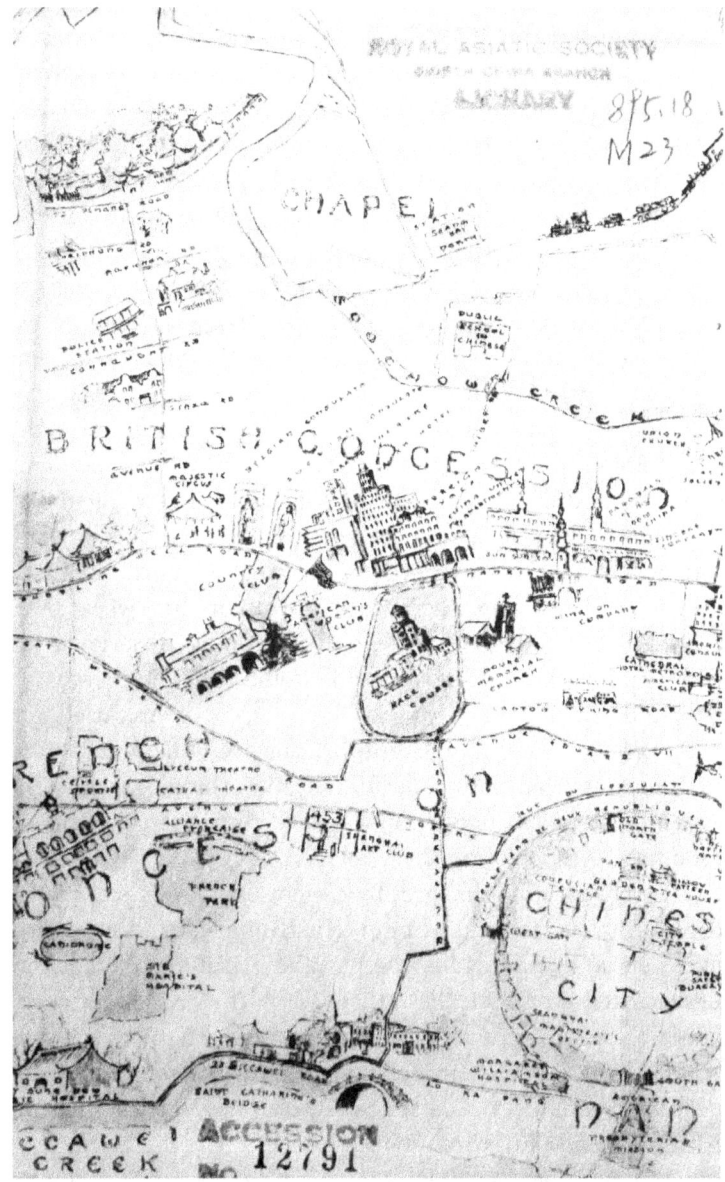

Figure 1: Mrs Alfred Dunlap, hand-drawn map of Shanghai, undated.

emotional, and creative activity.[4] Maps represent a set of knowledge, and as such they draw on the subjective nature of interpretation. This paper presents Florence Ayscough as another map-maker, charting knowledge of China that she accumulated over decades of living, studying, and travelling in the country. She herself was well aware of the subjective nature of this activity; we see her in the guise of ethnographer, explaining her methodologies, struggling to acquire language, questioning her own assumptions, interjecting her own experiences, and undertaking her task of reflecting "certain realities of Chinese life" with flair and humour.[5] The context for her work was the vast contemporary—and ongoing— enterprise of communicating knowledge of Chinese society to western audiences within such categories as ethnography, translations of literature, academic work undertaken for scholarly institutions such as the Royal Asiatic Society, travelogues and memoirs.[6] Ayscough's writings straddle the boundaries between academic discourse and popular exposition—during her lifetime she was acknowledged for the perspicacity of her scholarship, as well as for being an immensely accessible writer and lecturer. In part, this was due to a richly autobiographical strain in her work that allowed her to communicate a fresh, direct experience of Chinese nature and culture. She could, noted her second husband, Harley Farnsworth MacNair, have produced an outstanding formal autobiography; however, she didn't wish to take time from her cultural and philanthropic work to do so, and instead her publications and correspondence stand as an informal autobiography.[7]

The practice of ethnography cannot escape the subjective drive of its creators. As Kirsten Hastrup argues, "the reality experienced in the field is of a peculiar nature....It is not the unmediated world of the 'others', but the world **between** ourselves and the others."[8] The nature of Ayscough's mediation will be assessed here through a biography that focuses on her years in Shanghai, with particular reference to her NCBRAS activities, and then through a tighter focus on her account of building her home at 72 Penang Road—a piece of participant observation that allows her to reflect on her own interaction with place, culture and language.

EARLY CHILDHOOD IN SHANGHAI

Ayscough was born in Shanghai on January 20, 1875 to Thomas Reed Wheelock (1842-1920), a prominent Nova Scotia sea captain, and his Bostonian wife, Edith Haswell Clarke (1848-1913).[9] Wheelock had come to Shanghai in 1863 and joined the firm Wheelock and Company, where his brother John Andrew Wheelock was senior partner.[10] An 1855 map of Shanghai shows the Wheelock and Co. building on the Bund, just north of Canton Road.[11] T. R. Wheelock went on to establish the Shanghai Tug and Lighter Company, and became a wealthy and prominent member of the Shanghailander social circuit, as well as an accomplished sportsman, excelling in yachting and cross-country riding. Early Shanghai Hong directories provide the elliptical information that the family resided on Bubbling Well Road, and that Wheelock and Company functioned as "Auctioneers, Ship and Coal brokers, and Cargo Boat Proprietors." However, *Firecracker Land* (1932), a book she wrote for young adults, provides a rare evocation of an early Western childhood in Shanghai in the 1880s.[12] Of her father's river freight business, she recollected, "it was always exciting to watch busy steam launches towing the cargo boats—which look for all the world like black beetles."[13] She was born in the house that became the International Club[14], and experienced a childhood typical for her class and gender—relatively lonely, isolated, and spent in the company of animals such as her ponies and birds, rather than other children.[15] Her early education was desultory—she learnt French at a local convent, German from a governess, and basic literacy and numeracy from her mother. A great deal of her childhood was spent in the garden, which by the time she wrote *Firecracker Land* no longer existed:

> when I was small the garden seemed enormous. An oval drive led up to the great creamy-white house, covered with yellow roses. During the short season of their bloom, the gardeners cut them by the hundred. Every morning Mamma arranged them in shallow baskets, and they were piled into the trap in which Papa drove himself to the office. This was a high dogcart with red wheels, drawn by a stocky Mongolian pony. So every morning we watched it dash round the oval drive, and knew how busy Papa's office coolies were soon to be delivering the roses to our friends in Town.[16]

Recognizing the loneliness of their daughter, the Wheelocks brought her on the hunting and houseboat trips that were the popular recreational pursuits of privileged Shanghailanders.[17] Her recollections are rich in the sensory details that inform all her perceptions of China, and run throughout her ethnography as well as her translations. The autumn country landscape along the canal banks:

> had the deep purple brown of dead cotton stalks, in the winter it was the softer brown of old grass, and in the spring it was vivid with the yellow of rape and the pink of peach blossom.
> At night, curled under one of the famous red silk quilts, I would lie listening to the soft rhythmic thud of feet on the after deck as the crew swung to the *yu-lo*. The boat made scarcely a ripple as she cut through the dark glassy surface of the canal, but when she was drawn over a fish weir, the bamboos brushed under her keel with a most delicious *swish-sh-sh*.[18]

The Shanghai of her childhood was, of course, the already over-crowded city experiencing almost continual urban transformation and bouts of property speculation; but it was also a city surrounded by countryside, shooting districts and webs of canals. *Firecracker Land* opens boldly: "I was born in Shanghai. My earliest recollections are of the wide sky and sweeping plain of the Yangtze Valley."[19] It is the experience of nature rather than urbanity that informs her lifelong program of interpreting China to the west. The subjects that she alights on—garden design, historical travelogues, lyrical poetry, classical painting—are those that allow her to explore and transmit Chinese theories on the cultural significance of nature and landscape. And, alongside this intellectual enterprise, was the practical enterprise of designing environments that were physical expressions of these theories.

During Ayscough's childhood, the family paid several visits to North America. From 1889, when her father retired from China, she spent her adolescence in Boston, attending Mrs Quincy Shaw's School.[20] During this period she met Amy Lowell, who was to become a Pulitzer Prize winning poet, and a leading figure of the Imagist Movement. Their close lifelong friendship was to culminate, professionally, in the publication *Fir Flower Tablets* in 1921—translations from classical Chinese poets such as Li Po, Tu Fu and Wang Wei.

Ayscough's cosmopolitan childhood included trips to St. Andrews, New Brunswick, where her father established a summer cottage in 1897.[21] That year she returned to Shanghai, lived in a flat on the Bund, "dined, lunched and danced almost daily,"[22] rode cross-country on her pony and lived a life that by her own admission was "sheep-like" in its frivolity, insularity and ignorance of Chinese culture and language.[23] Like her father, she was a keen sportsperson all her life, and found in Shanghai the perfect milieu for her equestrian pursuits. A 1920 guidebook later pointed out that "There are few places where the adage 'The best thing for the inside of a man is the outside of a horse' is better understood than in Shanghai."[24] As a wealthy young woman of marriageable age, she participated in the upper echelons of Shanghai's social circuit and in its multifarious opportunities for sport and recreation. And, in a not atypical gesture of bravura for a privileged Western woman, she induced a male companion to take her to the walled Old City, where she reacted with the visceral fascination that shaped most touristic accounts of Shanghai's historic nucleus.[25]

That companion—soon to become her fiancé—was Francis Ayscouth, a British businessman from Malvern, working in Shanghai for the merchants Scott, Harding and Co.[26] The Winchester-educated Ayscough had come to China in 1882,[27] and at the time he met his future wife, was Master of the Paper Hunt—another bastion of Shanghailander social life.[28] During his Shanghai sojourn he belonged to the Shanghai Club, Country Club, and Race Club, and served on the Parks Committee, Municipal Council, was Chairman of the Shanghai Gas Co. and the Shanghai Horse Bazaar and Motor Co.[29]

THE NORTH CHINA BRANCH OF THE ROYAL ASIATIC SOCIETY: A CATALYST

Ayscough's marriage, at Trinity Church, Boston, on December 23, 1898, would seem to have cemented her identity within the Shanghailander establishment. However, over the next decades she was to transform into an internationally respected scholar on Chinese culture, a translator, educator, art patron and philanthropist. By her own account, her participation in the North China Branch of the Royal Asiatic Society was a significant factor in her intellectual growth. Although dissuaded by friends from learning Chinese, she began an *ad hoc* acquisition of the language in 1905.[30] By 1906 her name appeared on the membership list of the NCBRAS,[31] although in her autobiographical account in *Firecracker Land*, she conflates joining the society with becoming its Honorary Librarian in 1907. Her recollection of this event reveals the opportunities available at the time to enterprising and enthusiastic residents, despite lack of formal education or qualification:

> I went one day to the library of the society and the amiable young Chinese in charge allowed me, although I was not a member, to take away several valuable books. I tried in vain to find the library open that I might return them. I felt the books heavy on my conscience and, as he happened to take me in to dinner one night, told the secretary of the society [John C. Ferguson], a very learned gentleman indeed, of my plight.[32]

Over the ensuing conversation on books, Ayscough resolved "to join the society and read everything possible about China." Several days later, the British Consul General, Sir Pelham L. Warren—already a friend of the Ayscoughs—informed her that the council was offering her the position of Honorary Librarian and the task of re-cataloguing the library—a function she protested she knew nothing about. Warren's response, she recollected, was, "Neither do any of us, and you have more time to learn than we have!"[33]

The position of Honorary Librarian, which she filled until 1922, was to bring Ayscough great personal pleasure, as well as the opportunity to pursue her own research interests and assimilate the scholarship undertaken by society members and other sinologists. Under her leadership two editions of the library catalogue were published, in 1909 and 1921. By the 1920s the Society had built an impressive collection including rare books relating to Jesuit missionary activity in China; eighteenth-century prints; the seminal work of sinologists (many of them Royal Asiatic Society members) such as Paul Pelliot, James Legge, Robert Morrison; H.A. Giles, Emil Bretschneider; linguistic research and literary translations; the work of early western historians of Chinese art; as well as contemporary memoirs, travelogues and biographies. It was possible to browse from the Jesuit *Letters édifiantes et Curieuse Ecrites des Missions* to the *Shanghai Meteorological Society Reports*, to *An English Chinese Dictionary in Hakka Vernacular* to a *Map of the Waterways near Shanghai*. By her own account, this library was the major stimulus for her own investigations: "even though one cannot read all the books one catalogues, the mere handling of them brings an awareness of their being."[34] When she resigned this post she concluded, "I feel that through the doors of its library, I have been enabled to enter another world—a world in which the boundaries of time and space often seem annihilated. It has been my endeavor to hold open this door that others might enter."[35]

During the time of her council position, Ayscough was an active presence both in the Society, and in Shanghai's intellectual landscape. Her NCBRAS lecturing and publishing activities may be traced through the Society's journal—even after she left Shanghai in 1923—ranging among subjects as diverse as the Yangtze river's literary associations, Chinese poetry, holy mountains, the symbolism of the Forbidden City, and the City God cult.[36] She was an inspiring and entertaining speaker, often illustrating her talks with slides created from her own photographs, and in time came to treat lecturing as a true performance art.

Running throughout Ayscough's scholarship is reference to Chinese painting, and especially the interactions between painting and calligraphy. Again, she credited the NCBRAS for nurturing this expertise. In an article written for *The Mentor*, published in New York in 1918, she explained of her library position: "Through that office my interest in Chinese art and Chinese civilization was aroused, and I gave much of my time to study and observation."[37] Earlier, she had served on a committee with the art historian John C. Ferguson (the Society's Honorary Secretary and Journal Editor,) producing an exhibition of Chinese porcelain and art, presented by the Society at the Shanghai Mutual Telephone Company in November 1908.[38] Ferguson, who had originally come to China as an American missionary, went on to develop a career as an educator and governmental advisor, while simultaneously developing an expertise in Chinese art that enabled him to collect for major American institutions such as the Metropolitan Museum of Art, the Freer Gallery of Art and the Museum of Fine Arts, Boston.[39] As a friend and colleague, he seems to have had an impact on her connoisseurship, and doubtless encouraged Ayscough to develop her own connections with major American art museums.

The most ambitious of her early curatorial activities was her selection and documentation of a large collection of Chinese paintings exhibited in the China Pavilion, at the 1915 Panama-Pacific International Exposition in San Francisco. The embryo for this was a temporary exhibit organized in 1912 by the NCBRAS, of work from classical and modern periods by a Zhejiang Province collector, Liu Sung Fu.[40] Several of these paintings, including work by the innovative Shanghai School painter Ren Yi (1840-1896,) entered Ayscough's own collection and were donated to The Art Institute of Chicago by Ayscough's second husband, after her death *figure 2*.[41] At this time she also assisted Shanghai-based dealer E.A. Strehlneek with the production of an extensive illustrated catalogue[42]; Strehlneek focused on developing the foreign market for Chinese art, and indeed this collection was sold to a Stockholm collector.[43]

Ayscough's art history scholarship at this date was primarily a synthesis of existing sources, rather than original research. Artists' biographies and interpretive material were compiled from translations of Chinese sources, and the work of scholars such as Ferguson and Giles.[44] However, her agenda was to popularize a subject unfamiliar to a Western audience; the Panama-Pacific text, in particular, is explicative, employing an essentialist analysis contrasting Eastern and

Western mindsets to explain entirely different aesthetic qualities. Her approach—like that of Ferguson and Giles—is to frame art as expressive of cultural ideals. Landscape painting thus embodies a philosophical stance posited as opposite to that of the anthropomorphic West. For the Chinese painter, every natural thing plays "an active part of the great whole, of that Reality which is behind and beyond the flux of phenomena."[45] Giles had earlier written about differences in Eastern and Western views of nature, but in Ayscough's words we might find echoes of the American Transcendentalism that certainly influenced her maternal ancestors.[46]

Figure 2: Ren Yi, *The Five Relationships*, 1895. Hanging scroll, ink and colours on paper, 149.2 x 81.3 cm. Gift of Florence Ayscough and Harley Farnsworth MacNair, 1943.133. Reproduction, The Art Institute of Chicago.

Ayscough's connoisseurship was much further refined through her own collecting activities; these were significantly shaped by an initially disquieting event. In 1917 a compradore in her husband's firm had embezzeled a substantial sum of money; as recompense, Ayscough attempted to sell his collection of paintings and calligraphy in the United States, using the museum and art connections she had been developing.[47] She exhibited at Gertrude Vanderbilt Whitney's Studio, and showed the modern pieces at The Art Institute of Chicago, lectured on these works and successfully placed some with collectors;[48] the rest remained in her collection, and were eventually donated to the Art Institute of Chicago.[49] She was later to explain how this business difficulty had sharpened her appreciation: "My studies in Chinese art had taught me to appreciate in full measure the extraordinary interest of the art treasure that had come into my possession. With this wonderful assemblage of exquisite examples of old Chinese art I was able to develop my own knowledge of the subject..."[50]

In preparation for her lectures, she translated some of the calligraphic scrolls, and shared these with Amy Lowell—the genesis of the translation project that resulted in the publication of *Fir Flower Tablets* in 1921. As Lowell knew no Chinese, Ayscough, in collaboration with her Chinese tutor in Shanghai, Nung Chu, provided the foundation. As Lowell explained in her preface: "Mrs. Ayscough would first write out the poem in Chinese. Not in the Chinese characters, of course, but in transliteration. Opposite every word she put the various meanings of it which accorded with its place in the text, since I could not use a Chinese dictionary. She also gave the analyses of whatever characters seemed to her to require it."[51]

Fir Flower Tablets may be thought of in at least three distinct ways. First, this book can be situated within the Modernist experimentation with Eastern forms and subject matter; Pound's *Cathay* (1915), based on the earlier translations of Ernest Fenollosa, is the obvious parallel. Second, it takes its place within a contemporary body of academic translation;[52] Waley's work of the late teens and early twenties is contemporaneous with *Fir Flower Tablets*, and Waley was a figure referenced often in the Ayscough/Lowell correspondence.[53] And third, this publication may be seen as perpetuating Ayscough's ethnographic enterprise of interpreting Chinese culture to the West.[54] In terms of its translation methods and literary merit, it received mixed reviews on publication, and continues to attract divergent critical opinion.[55] However, its worth in terms of providing a cultural context for Western readers was—and still is—acknowledged.[56] *Fir Flower Tablets* was another "map" for Western readers, and it is significant that Ayscough was particularly concerned about the map that comprised the book's frontispiece.[57] A piece of calligraphy, and the floor plan to a Chinese house, were the other illustrations.

Ayscough wrote a lengthy introduction to *Fir Flower*

Tablets to help situate her readers through a description of China's topography, climate, and political and social history. In theory, this would enable a reader to more fully appreciate a line such as the following from Li Po's "Parrot Island": "The mists part and one can see the leaves of the spear-orchid, and its scent is warm on the wind."[58] In her introduction, she had supplied the following information on this orchid [*lan hua*]:

> A small epidendrum, translated in this book as 'spear-orchid.' It is a symbol for noble men and beautiful, refined women. Confucius compared the *Chün Tzǔ*, Princely or Superior Man, to this little orchid with its delightful scent. In poetry, it is also used in reference to the Women's Apartments and everything connected with them, suggesting, as it does, the extreme of refinement.[59]

However, Ayscough's knowledge of *lan hua* extended far beyond its symbolism. In a chapter on gardens in *A Chinese Mirror* she reveals more direct experience:

> The great interest lies in the strangely varied petals of this tiny flower. In competitions, prizes are given for novelties. Each year at the shows held in the Shanghai City the pre-eminent plant is raised on a high stand in the centre of the hall[...]
>
> In the *lan hua* season those who love the flowers send many *li* along the water-ways to meet the boats of *lan hua* gatherers coming from the hills , and often buy a whole boatload in the hope of discovering a novelty.[60]

And it was Ayscough's direct experience of nature in China, and her observational acuity, that brought such diversity of natural species, nuance of colour and textural depth to the Ayscough/Lowell translations. In terms of flora and fauna, *Fir Flower Tablets* is a species-rich celebration of the natural world. In a letter to the *China Journal* (the publication of the Shanghai Museum) Ayscough notes their ornithological precision:

I find that in our collection of one hundred and thirty-seven pieces, among the birds referred to are: kites, vultures, nightingales, yellow geese, wild geese, magpies, orioles, swallows, parrots, white herons, yellow herons, mandarin ducks, jackdaws, gulls, pheasants, cocks and chickens, to say nothing of the fabulous birds such as the Silver-crested Love Pheasant, the Green Fire-bird, and the Jade Love-bird.[61]

Conversely, it was a perceived lack of ornithological accuracy that attracted one of Ayscough's few negative public comments on Waley. His mistranslation of a line suggesting that the poet *saw* (rather than heard) the reclusive golden oriole was, according to Ayscough, "a mistake which every naturalist would condemn." While she acknowledged that although Waley—who had never been to China—could produce "exquisite" poetry, he lacked "a certain vividness of perception, a vividness which only a visual experience of China could give him."[62]

As an example of the vividness Ayscough could bring, one example from her collaboration with Lowell—Wang Wei's "Blue Green Stream"—may suffice:

Every time I have started for the Yellow Flower River,
I have gone down the Blue-Green Stream,
Following the hills, making ten thousand turnings
We go along rapidly, but advance scarcely one hundred *li*.
We are in the midst of a noise of water,
Of the confused and mingled sounds of water broken by stones,
And in the deep darkness of pine-trees.Rocked, rocked,
Moving on and on,
We float past water-chestnuts
Into a still clearness reflecting reeds and rushes.
My heart is clean and white as silk; it has already achieved Peace;
It is smooth as the placid river.I long to stay here, curled up on the rocks,
Dropping my fish-line forever.[63]

A comparison with Witter Bynner's translation of the same poem (Bynner visited, rather than lived in, China) underscores the sensory richness of the Ayscough/Lowell version:

I have sailed the River of Yellow Flowers,
Borne by the channel of a green stream,
Rounding ten thousand turns through the mountains
On a journey of less than thirty miles....
Rapids hum over heaped rocks;
But where light grows dim in the thick pines,
The surface of an inlet sways with nut-horns
And weeds are lush along the banks.
...Down in my heart I have always been as pure
As this limpid water is....
Oh, to remain on a broad flat rock,
And to cast a fishing-line forever![64]

In the first version, the still water reflecting rushes, and calmness of a heart "clean and white as silk" may well be echoes of childhood experience on Chinese houseboats. In short, *Fir Flower Tablets* depended on the fact of Florence Ayscough's life in China—not just in terms of her absorption in language and access to a teacher, but also for her sensitivity to the natural world she encountered there.

THE GRASS HUT AT YELLOW REACH...OR 72 PENANG ROAD

Even by those who value her scholarly contributions, Ayscough has been accused of Romanticism.[65] On the surface, her account of building her *pied à terre* "grass hut" in the garden of her Shanghai mansion house, might seem to bear out this accusation. *A Chinese Mirror* (1925), which contains this account, was very positively received, yet it was acceded that some might argue she "poeticized the dinginess and dirt completely out of sight."[66] A lengthy chapter of *A Chinese Mirror* is devoted to describing the building of The Grass Hut; far from being simply a light, lyrical journey through folk customs, this text is Ayscough at her best, interpreting China through close observation, explication, and the continual thread of autobiography.

In 1922 the Ayscoughs were preparing to retire from China, yet "felt the need of some little place which could await the comings and goings of future years, so built the Grass Hut which is always ready for our use."[67] Two decades earlier, the Ayscoughs had built a house close to the boundary of the 1899 International Settlement extension, where there would be room for extensive gardens. The site—60 Gordon Road, named Wild Goose Happiness House—was at the intersection of the current Anyuan and Jiangning Roads, close to Suzhou Creek. This had been "as much like an American house as possible."[68] By 1922 the Ayscoughs had decided to sell this substantial property, yet retain a small parcel of the grounds for the construction of a Chinese courtyard house and garden. During the construction period, from summer 1922, Ayscough kept a journal, which provided the basis for her published account. Her text is accompanied by reproductions of graphically striking drawings by Lucille Douglass (1876-1935), an Alabama-born artist Ayscough met in Shanghai. The two women enjoyed a long friendship and prolific working relationship; Douglass illustrated a number of Ayscough's texts and hand-coloured her lecture slides, while Ayscough offered patronage, support, and the promotion of Douglass' career in the Unites States.[69]

This text is, in many ways, a classic piece of ethnography, utilizing the fieldwork methods of close and sustained observation, diary-keeping, the selection of native informants, transcription of conversations, and inclusion of visual material such as drawings and a floor plan. She is emphatic in her claim that "it is to be like the cottages of Kiangsu [Jiangsu], and ...I want to observe all time-honoured customs while it is being built."[70] Through the course of the text Ayscough leads us through the process of construction: the roles and activities of the workmen from senior foreman to young apprentice; the layout and decoration of the architectural elements; the design of the garden; and the decoration of the interior. However, beyond providing a catalogue of observations, she provides what Geertz was much later to describe as "thick description," presenting for the reader not just the behaviors themselves, but the cultural contexts that help shape these behaviors.[71]

For example, the action of raising the richly carved ridge pole was surrounded by ceremonies, singing, prescribed offerings to Lu Pan (the saint of carpenters,) and gift-giving. All of this is intimately described, then made legible to a western audience through an analysis of belief systems and language. The critical reception of *A Chinese Mirror* indicates that this agenda was understood by her readers—including those residing in China who could observe first-hand what Ayscough interpreted. For instance, the missionary publication *The Chinese Recorder* noted that "page after page is filled with accounts of the meaning and origin of many of the apparently *meaningless* [my italics] customs which go on all about us daily."[72]

Confident in her role as interpreter, she also acknowledges that such investigation is rife with the difficulties that arise from cross-cultural communication. She is aware, often with great humour, of the biases and assumptions that come from being situated as a Western woman in semi-colonial Shanghai. For example, she recollects an earlier tale involving her home's "Lonely Spirits" – the generations of "intangible wraiths" residing in spirit tablets left behind by the property's previous occupants:

> Being very young at the time and utterly inexperienced, I suggested that the decorative ancestral hall with its precious contents be placed intact in our vestibule. The look which came over Canton Carpenter's face did more to enlighten the darkness of my ignorance than any torrent of words could have accomplished.[73]

As a compromise, a shrine was built in the garden to house the spirit tablets and Ayscough's staff ensured "the proper sacrifices" were offered at "the appointed times."

Now, she wonders what the builders of her Grass Hut are singing, then recounts the tale of a friend who met a conventionally attractive violet-eyed, golden-haired Western woman beside another construction site. The foreman's extempore verse ran: "Her eyes are like an old blue coat....Like an old blue coat, a beggar would throw away." Throughout her writings Ayscough makes liberal use of direct quotations—a common ethnographic tactic to convey legitimacy; of course, in terms of authenticity these are doubly removed from their original contexts as we receive the words of workmen, servants, and, especially her esteemed teacher Nung Chu, second-hand via her own translations. Her writings exhibit a noticeable degree of self awareness and sensitivity as to the difficulty of the enthographer's enterprise, yet for Ayscough her "Chinese Mirror" offers her a relatively unclouded reflection. The "pervasive nervousness about the whole business of claiming to explain enigmatical others on the grounds that you have gone about with them in their native habitat" was by the 1920s, still decades in the future.[74]

Figure 3: Lucille Douglass, drawing of garden at 72 Penang Rd., Shanghai, reproduced in A Chinese Mirror.

What she does accomplish, though, is an explanation of herself, and the "liberal education" received through building this house.[75] The Grass Hut is a repository for her own learning. The house's name is a tribute to Tu Fu, who built his own "Grass Hut" in Chengdu. Over the previous years, Ayscough had been translating Tu Fu's poetry for a two-volume "autobiography" of Tu Fu she was to write after she left Shanghai. Like Ayscough's, his was no primitive shelter, but a comfortable family home.[76] Images of other poets and historical figures of significance to her are carved on the home's woodwork.

The home's garden is a demonstration of her education in the aesthetics and botanical contents of classical Chinese gardens figure 3. (One chapter of *A Chinese Mirror* is dedicated to this subject.) The Grass Hut is a showcase for treasured gifts of plants such as a grass with tuberous roots she identifies as book girdle grass, given to her by a local tailor; she describes this plant's literary history, as well as its role in traditional medicine. The narrative moves through the spaces of her courtyards, alighting on species cultivated in Chinese gardens such as magnolia, osmanthus, paulownia, azalea, plum, bamboo, and a gnarled pine likened by Nung Chu to "a Buddhist priest or a Daoist."[77]

While botany and horticulture were personal and lifelong interests (she created gardens in all of her major residences), they were also shared and amplified by the activities of the NCBRAS, whose journals are rich in botanical investigation. For example, sinologist Emil Bretschneider had published his encyclopedic "Botanicon Sinicum: Notes on Chinese Botany from Native and Western Sources" in a three part series between 1881 and 1895.[78] Ayscough later referenced Bretschneider in her translations of Tu Fu.[79] Although not the most remarked-upon aspect of concession-era life, an intense interest in the natural environment was nevertheless one thread of Western residents' activities, increasingly promoted through the activities of the Society, the museum it had opened in 1874, and the museum publication *The China Journal*.[80]

The Grass Hut was also a site to gather and display memories of travel in China. On a trip to the ruins of the Old Summer Palace in Beijing (Yuanmingyuan), destroyed by Anglo-French troops in 1860, Ayscough had gathered shards of brilliantly coloured tile she arranged in her garden courtyard.[81] The dragon wall that snaked around the corner of this courtyard was, in its symbolism, a reference both to the Forbidden City and to a garden closer to home, the Yuyuan in Shanghai's Old City, described in much detail later in *A Chinese Mirror*.[82]

In addition to travel memories, Ayscough's art collection

was displayed in the house. A prized ink rubbing hung above a fireplace *figure 4*.[83] The Guest Hall was furnished with Chinese chairs, and a pair of Ming dynasty lacquered book cupboards.[84] She also mentions the accoutrements of the scholar's study, such as a bamboo brush holder, and a set of seals. Much can be learned about her collecting activities from a major donation to the Art Institute of Chicago in 1943, selections of which are still displayed in special exhibitions.[85]

Figure 4: Lucille Douglass, drawing of interior of 72 Penang Rd., Shanghai, reproduced in A Chinese Mirror.

This gift included traditional and contemporary paintings, calligraphy, ink rubbings, textiles and porcelain—noteably a jar given to her by the Empress Dowager Cixi. While not all of these works can be documented as having been collected during the Shanghai years, it is probable—given the collecting activities she discusses in her writings—that the bulk was acquired during this period. The Grass Hut, then, expressed her activities as scholar and collector; its creation was a means to communicate the body of knowledge and aesthetic development she had so assiduously acquired over the past two decades.

However, in a passage of self-deprecating humour she also affirms her identity as a Western resident of Shanghai, conditioned to privileges and conveniences entirely foreign to a rural retreat. On one page she writes "I continually reiterate that it is to be like the cottages of Kiangsu,"[86] but on the next she includes a plan of a spacious and well-staffed western home, with bathrooms attached to each bedroom, a central heating furnace room, a smoking room and a pantry *figure*

5.[87] She elaborates:

> It is difficult to preserve a completely Chinese interior when one must introduce that Occidental comfort of which I have already spoken. Fire-places for instance are entirely exotic to a Kiangsu cottage. I have tried to mitigate the delightful evil by framing ours in a flat round circle. Lights have been cleverly concealed by the electrician in old Chinese fittings. There are beautiful candelabra, and black iron hanging baskets formerly used to hold both flowers and candles. Bright silk

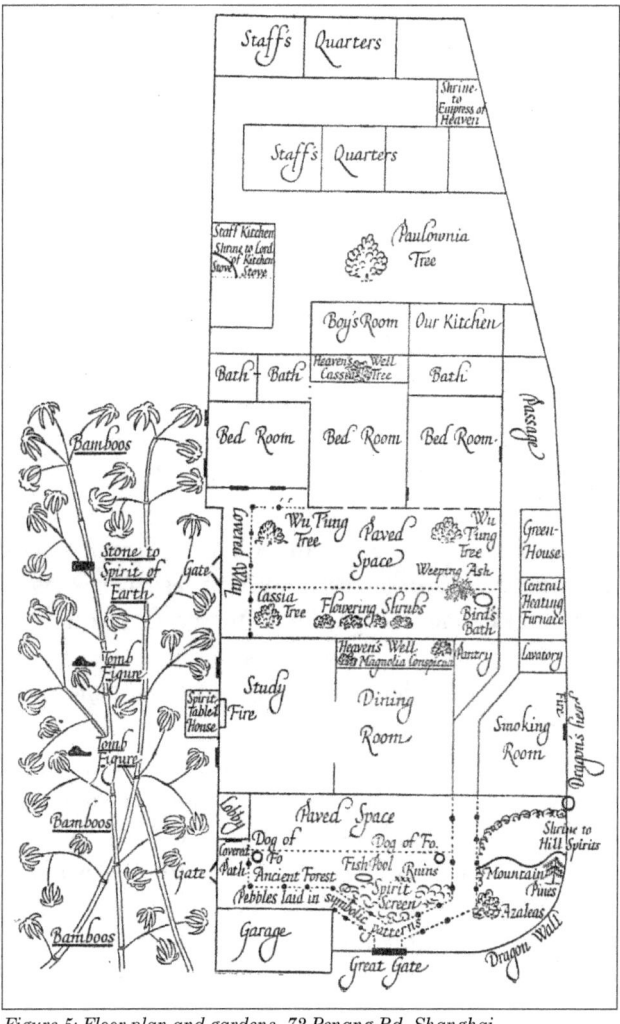

Figure 5: Floor plan and gardens, 72 Penang Rd, Shanghai.

51

tassels, yellow, green, purple and scarlet, hang from all light fixtures and the colours blend most effectively.

This house was a passage of autobiography, encompassing North American origins, Shanghailander identity, and the negotiations of the ethnographer straddling cultures.

CONSOLIDATING A CAREER

Following Francis Ayscough's retirement, the couple sailed from Shanghai in April 1923, and arrived in Canada in May, settling in St. Andrews, New Brunswick where Thomas Wheelock had established a large summer home.[88] They brought with them from China 43 cases of household goods and books.[89] Ayscough also brought with her the research and papers she had been compiling in Shanghai that were to provide the basis for her future scholarship. Her output over the following years was prodigious, and included the books *A Chinese Mirror* (1925), *The Autobiography of a Chinese Dog* (1926), a two-volume work on Tu Fu (1929, 1934), *Firecracker Land* (1932), *Chinese Women, Yesterday and Today* (1937), as well as articles in the NCBRAS journal, and appearances on the international lecture circuit. Francis Ayscough had become seriously ill, and the couple traveled widely— London, Switzerland, Austria and Guernsey—seeking medical treatment. During these trips, Florence Ayscough took the opportunity to lecture and further her professional reputation.[90] She became acclaimed as an engaging speaker, often donning "oriental" costume for these performances.[91] (One of her kimonos now belongs to the Charlotte County Museum in St. Stephen, New Brunswick.)[92]

If she was popularly considered "brilliant", she was also acknowledged as authoritative. In 1921 the NCBRAS had elected her to the position of "Honorary Member" –she was the first woman to receive this title, and took her place among sinologists such as H. A. Giles, Henri Cordier, Paul Pelliot, and Sir J. H. Stewart Lockhart.[93] In 1926 she was elected to the Society of Woman Geographers.[94] In 1927 she was elected a member of the Royal Geographical Society;[95] Acadia University in Nova Scotia, awarded her an Honorary D. Litt. the same year.[96] In 1931 she was elected to the American

Oriental Society;[97] and in 1932 to the Royal Anthropological Institute of Great Britain and Ireland.[98]

Reviews of her written work and appearances suggest she successfully persuaded her audiences that she was offering a privileged, tactile and immediate (as well as culturally elevated) insight into an exotic culture:

> She tells of another China, not the one we know. Instead of bandits and missionaries, plagues, and famines, revolutions and wily mandarins, she writes of peace and romance, beauty and color. She takes one into secret gardens, silent temples, ancient palaces hidden away from eyes of the curious; along strange gray rivers, among people who love beauty and a quiet life.[99]

Even when ventriloquising her dog Yo Fei she was commended for her "comprehension of the reality", and for offering readers "the opportunity to live in the country for a time."[100] Of course, Yo Fei's reality was instead Ayscough's reality, with its intense focus on personal sensory experience. Although not on the surface a promising read, this book gives access to a different facet of Ayscough's private domestic experience—the summer trips to Wei Hai Wei, the names of her cats (Curzon and Kitchener), the rituals of teatime under the camphor tree at Gordon Road, the parties in the garden, her practice of photography, the pattern of a favourite tea set, her bout of typhoid. And, as with *Firecracker Land*, the semi-rural outskirts of Shanghai are intimately described. In spring the kites were like "great centipedes waving in the air." And, "the willows burst their buds and Winter wheat painted the fields leaf green". A favorite walk leads them along Suzhou Creek, with its cotton mills, silk mills, factories, and 10,000 boats.[101]

A freshness of response to the natural world is one reason Ayscough felt such affinity with the poets Li Po and Tu Fu. When she describes the former as a "sensuous realist" she may as well be describing herself. And her empathy with the latter resulted in a still acclaimed "autobiography" of the poet that is rich in her own autobiographical reflection. Interspersed with her translations of Tu Fu's poems are digressions on qualities of landscape, or conversations with Nung Chu about different types of chrysanthemum:

> and from that day the hours of translation were punctuated, as the clock struck eleven, by sweet chrysanthemum tea served in cups from the Imperial dinner- service which I was fortunate enough to acquire some years ago. The straw-coloured drink is delicious, but I think its flavour was enhanced for me by the thought that I was sipping the self-same potion that Tu Fu had sipped so long ago. It made a liquid link, if I may so express it, down the centuries.[102]

In her selection of Tu Fu's poems, Ayscough as a collector of textiles seems to have deliberately chosen several with a textile theme. For example, "White Silk Thread" is a detailed description of silk garment production:

> I grieve that, following the fashion of the time, this
> plain raw silk is already dyed;
> When cut from the creaking loom its colour was
> A ray of light.
> Lovely women consider it carefully; use the fire-
> Filled iron to make it smooth;
> Cut out, sew their garments, on which all traces of
> Thread and needle are invisible.[103]

SHANGHAI AND CHICAGO: A NCBRAS LOVE AFFAIR

Following Francis Ayscough's death on Guernsey in December 1933, Florence Ayscough returned to Shanghai in the spring of 1934 for an extended visit. She again became active in the activities of the NCBRAS, serving as Honorary Consulting Librarian and also lecturing.[104] At this point, the narrative returns to the NCBRAS library, where in 1916 she met a young scholar, Harley Farnsworth MacNair (1891-1947). By his own admission he fell in love and remained so:

> From that bright autumnal afternoon in 1916, when she opened the door of the library in the old Royal Asiatic Society

building on Museum Road, crossed the room to me (I was using the card catalogue), and said in that exquisite voice, "Good afternoon! I am Mrs. Ayscough; can I help you in any way?" and added, "I am Honorary Librarian of the R.A.S.," I have loved her.[105]

MacNair had first come to Shanghai in 1912, and served on faculty at St. John's University. He eventually became Head of the Department of History and Government. The membership lists of the NCBRAS indicate that he became a life member in 1920. MacNair spent the years until 1927 mostly in China, then after a year in Seattle became Professor of Far Eastern History and Institutions at the University of Chicago. In China he had visited Ayscough often; he maintained his friendship after her departure, visiting her in Chicago, St. Andrews and Guernsey.[106] MacNair was in Shanghai in 1934, and that autumn took a steamer trip up the Yangtze with Ayscough, followed by a trip to Japan in spring 1935.[107] That spring both MacNair and Ayscough delivered lectures to the Society.[108] They were married on Guernsey on September 7, 1935—an outcome that seemed felicitously inevitable, but one that surprised American colleagues. A piqued notice in *The New York Times* remarked that his friends and associates "learned of the marriage through a copy of a Guernsey newspaper."[109]

The couple settled in Chicago, calling their home at 5533 Woodlawn Avenue, The House of the Wutung Trees, after the painting by Ren Yi that Ayscough had catalogued back in 1915 for the Panama Pacific International Exposition. Much of the couple's art collections were housed here, including the "dogs of Fo" that had guarded the "Grass Hut".[110] Their collecting activities continued during a 1939 trip to China, where they acquired decorative arts, pottery, and calligraphy.[111] In June MacNair lectured to the NCBRAS.[112] The couple's Chicago house was recognized as a "treasure house, museum, and library, a scholar's workshop, as well as a hearth and home."[113] Here, Florence Ayscough continued her work of interpreting China to the West, almost until her death in April 1942.

POSTSCRIPT: FLUX

The house and garden on Nanjing Road (W.) where Ayscough spent her childhood have been obliterated; the district is affluently commercial. The enormous gardens of Wild Goose Happiness House, with their camphor trees under which Ayscough took afternoon tea, are gone. The Jade Buddha Temple, which was being constructed nearby, and with whose priests she was on friendly terms, is still bustling with tourists and pilgrims. The intersection on which the Grass Hut stood is typical of the terrain of early twenty-first century Shanghai—the saffron walls of the temple sweep round one corner, there are lane houses, small stores, an enormous construction site cordoned with barbed wire, an anonymous blue-glassed office building. It won't look the same next year. Indeed it changed very quickly after the Ayscoughs departed—Shanghai has been briskly re-mapping itself for decades. The Desk Hong directories list the MacNairs at 72 Penang Road in 1936; there is a gap in 1937, and by 1938 the New Shanghai Construction Company occupied this address. From the mid 1930s Penang Road became increasingly industrialized, and with the addition of lane houses, ever-more densely populated.

Florence Ayscough would have been unsurprised, knowing well that "A flower face endures but a short season".[114]

Endnotes

1. The Shanghai Library owns an extensive collection of Shanghai maps, including over 1,000 pre-1949 foreign language maps. The North China Branch of the Royal Asiatic Society was a major source of this material. Recent conceptual mapping projects include Yang Guangnan's "Map-drawing—Art in School 2008, a subjective map produced at the Xinguang School for Migrant Workers' Children.
2. Harley Farnsworth MacNair, ed., *Florence Ayscough & Amy Lowell: Correspondence of a Friendship* (Chicago: University of Chicago Press, 1945) endpapers.
3. Ayscough's second husband, Harley Farnsworth MacNair, describes the process of making this map from an original watercolour: MacNair, *Correspondence* 10.

4. For a discussion of cartography as the focus of critical attention see, for example, Denis Cosgrove, ed., *Mappings* (London: Reaktion Books, 2002).
5. Florence Ayscough, *A Chinese Mirror: Being Reflections of the Reality behind Appearance* (London: Jonathan Cape Ltd., 1925) 10.
6. For a selection of these writings, see Francis Wood, *The Lure of China: Writers from Marco Polo to J.G. Ballard* (Hong Kong: Joint Publishing Co. Ltd. and Yale University Press, 2009.)
7. Harley Fransworth MacNair, ed., *The Incomparable Lady: Tributes and Other Memorabilia Pertaining to Florence Wheelock Ayscough MacNair* (Chicago: privately printed, 1946) 3. I am grateful to Peter Sanger for making this material available to me.
8. Kirsten Hastrup, "Writing Ethnography," *Anthropology and Autobiography*, ed. Judith Okely and Helen Callaway (New York: Routledge, 1992) 117.
9. Ayscough's birth date is contested; according to some sources she was born in 1878. However, Ayscough's second husband supplied the date 1875—a fact stressed by Peter Sanger in his excellent biographical material on Ayscough: Peter Sanger, *White Salt Mountain: Words in Time* (Kentville, Nova Scotia, 2005). Biographical details on Ayscough's parents may be found in Catherine MacKenzie, "Florence Wheelock Ayscough's Niger Reef Tea House," *The Journal of Canadian Art History* 23. 1-2 (2002): 37, 55.
10. This and following biographical details from the Obituary notice for Thomas Reed Wheelock, *North China Herald* 10 Jan.1920: 86.
11. Map reproduced in F. L. Hawks Pott, *A Short History of Shanghai* (Shanghai: Kelly and Walsh, Ltd., 1928) 120 facing.
12. Florence Ayscough, *Firecracker Land: Pictures of the Chinese World for Younger Readers* (New York: Houghton Mifflin Company, 1932).
13. Ayscough, *Firecracker Land* 3.
14. My thanks to Peter Hibbard, who identifies the site of Ayscough's first Shanghai home as the current 722 Nanjing Road (W).
15. In *Firecracker Land*, Ayscough refers to her younger brother, Geoffrey (d. 1920) and also mentions a younger sister, Marjorie,

who seems to have died in infancy or early childhood.
16. Ayscough, *Firecracker Land* 3.
17. For a contemporary evocation of this pursuit, see J.O.P. Bland, *Houseboat Days in China* (London: Edward Arnold, 1909).
18. Ayscough, *Firecracker Land* 15-17.
19. Ayscough, *Firecracker Land* 3.
20. Ayscough, *Firecracker Land* 19-20; Peter Sanger, *White Salt Mountain: Words in Time* (Kentville, Nova Scotia: Gaspereau Press, Ltd., 2005) 34.
21. Sanger 37.
22. Ayscough, *Firecracker Land* 23.
23. For an excoriating account of Shanghailander mentality, see Robert Bickers, "Shanghailanders: The Formation and Identity of the British Settler Community in Shanghai 1843-1937," *Past and Present* 159 (May 1998): 161-211.
24. C. E. Darwent, *Shanghai: A Handbook for Travellers and Residents* (Shanghai: Kelly and Walsh, Ltd., 1920) 168.
25. For example, a near contemporaneous account is supplied by Eliza Ruhamah Scidmore, *China, the Long-Lived Empire*. New York: Century, 1900.
26. Marriage notice, *Boston Daily Globe* 24 Dec.,1898: 6.
27. Carroll Lunt, ed. *The China Who's Who 1922* (Shanghai: Kelly and Walsh, Ltd., 1922) 31.
28. Frances Ayscough was Master of the Paper Hunt 1897-98. See Charles N. Davis, *A History of the Shanghai Paper Hunt 1863-1930* (Shanghai: Kelly and Walsh, Ltd., 1930) 37.
29. *China Who's Who* 31.
30. Ayscough, *Firecracker Land* 32.
31. *Journal of the North China Branch of the Royal Asiatic Society* (JNCBRAS) 37 (1906).
32. Ayscough, *Firecracker Land* 35-6.
33. Ayscough, *Firecracker Land* 36..
34. Ayscough, *Firecracker Land* 37.
35. Librarian's report, *JNCBRAS* 54 (1923): vii.
36. Ayscough published the following long articles in the *JNCBRAS*: "Shrines of history: Peak of the East –T'ai Shan," *JNCBRAS* 48 (1917): 57-70; "Chinese Poetry and its Connotations," *JNCBRAS* 51 (1920): 99-134; "Notes on the symbolism of the Purple Forbidden City," *JNCBRAS*

52 (1921): 51-78; "Preliminary Notes on the Literary Background of 'The Great River',",*JNCBRAS* 54 (1923): 129-149; "Cult of the Ch'eng Huang Lao Yeh (Spiritual Magistrate of the City Walls and Moats)" *JNCBRAS* 55 (1924): 131-155; "The Symbolism of the Forbidden City, Peking," *JNCBRAS* 61 (1930): 111-126.
37. Florence Ayscough, "Chinese Painting," *The Mentor* 6.20 (1918): 12.
38. *JNCBRAS* 40 (1909): 113.
39. In the field of education, Ferguson was instrumental in founding the Nanyang Gongxue in Shanghai, which was to become Jiao Tong University.
40. Florence Ayscough, *Catalogue of Chinese Paintings Ancient and Modern by Famous Masters. The Property of Mr. Liu Sung Fu* (Shanghai: The Oriental Press, 1914).
41. I am grateful to Elinor Pearlstein, Associate Curator of Chinese Art, The Art Institute of Chicago, for providing this information.
42. E.A. Strehlneek, *Chinese Pictorial Art* (Shanghai: The Commercial Press, 1914).
43. The frontispiece to this book notes this sale; artwork with a documented Strehlneek provenance, such as the pieces catalogued in *Chinese Pictorial Art*, is periodically sold through international auction.
44. See, for example, H.A. Giles, *History of Chinese Pictorial Art (* Shanghai: Kelly and Walsh, Ltd., 1905).
45. Ayscough, *Catalogue of Chinese Paintings*, 5.
46. Mackenzie draws out the numerous contacts between the Clarke family and the American Transcendentalists in *Niger Reef Tea House*, 55.
47. MacNair, *Correspondence* 18.
48. Art Institute of Chicago exhibition archives list the "Modern Chinese Paintings, Florence Ayscough Collection," June 1918, 14 April 2009 <http://www.artic.edu/aic/libraries/research/specialcollections/aic/exhibitions/1910/1918.html>. Her article in *The Mentor* illustrates some pieces that had been sold to private collectors.
49. MacNair, *Correspondence* 58. MacNair's footnote explains the subsequent history of these remaining works.

50. Ayscough, *Mentor* 12.
51. Florence Ayscough and Amy Lowell, *Fir Flower Tablets: Poems from the Chinese* (Boston: Houghton Mifflin Company, 1921) ix.
52. The quality of the translations in *Fir Flower Tablets* was still considered "very good" by Kenneth Rexroth in 1971, while Ayscough's individual translations of Tu Fu he found "excellent". Kenneth Rexroth, *One Hundred Poems from the Chinese* (New York: New Directions Books, 1971) 146.
53. For example, Arthur Waley, *A Hundred and Seventy Poems from the Chinese* (London: Constable, 1918).
54. Yunte Huang argues for an ethnographic reading of *Fir Flower Tablets* in *Transpacific Displacement: Ethnography, Translation, and Intertextual Travel in Twentieth-Century American Literature* (Berkeley: University of California Press: 2002) 52.
55. Mari Yoshihara, for example, is critical of what she identifies as outworn patterns of gender and sexuality in *Embracing the East: White Women and American Orientalism* (New York: Oxford University Press, 2003). From a poet's perspective, Peter Sanger provides a lengthy, often positive analysis of the Ayscough/Lowell enterprise in *White Salt Mountain*.
56. See Richard Le Galliene, "A Caravan from China Comes," rev. of *Fir Flower Tablets* by Florence Ayscough and Amy Lowell, *The New York Times* 15 Jan. 1922: 4, 21; and more currently Huang, *Transpacific Displacement*.
57. She mentions this map on many occasions through her correspondence with Lowell.
58. Ayscough and Lowell, *Fir Flower Tablets* 61.
59. Ayscough and Lowell, *Fir Flower Tablets* lvii.
60. Ayscough, *Mirror* 230-1.
61. Florence Ayscough, correspondence, *China Journal* 2.6 (Nov. 1924): 528-9.
62. Florence Ayscough, rev. of *More Translations from the Chinese* by Arthur Waley, *The Chinese Recorder* (May 1920): 354.
63. Ayscough and Lowell, *Fir Flower Tablets* 123.
64. Witter Bynner and Kiang Kang-Hu, The Jade Mountain: A Chinese Anthology (New York: Alfred Knopf, 1931) 179.
65. See, for example, Jinhua Emma Teng, "A Construction of the

'Traditional Chinese Woman' in the Western Academy: A Critical Review." *Signs* 22.1 (Autumn 1996): 122.
66. Rev. of *A Chinese Mirror: Being Reflections of the Reality behind Appearance* by Florence Ayscough, *The Chinese Recorder* (July 1926): 516.
67. Ayscough, *Mirror* 19.
68. Ayscough, *Firecracker Land* 30.
69. Mackenzie includes a detailed account of Douglass' life and her collaboration with Ayscough in "Niger Reef Teahouse".
70. Ayscough, *Mirror* 25.
71. This is discussed in the classic text, Clifford Geertz, *The Interpretation of Cultures: Selected Essays* (New York: Basic Books, 1973).
72. *Recorder* 517.
73. Ayscough, *Mirror* 53.
74. An anxiety voiced by Geertz, *Works and Lives: The Anthropologist as Author* (Stanford: Stanford University Press, 1988) 130-1.
75. Ayscough, *Mirror* 19.
76. David Hinton, trans., *The Selected Poems of Tu Fu* (New York: New Directions Books, 1989) 126.
77. Ayscough, *Mirror* 76.
78. Emil Bretschneider, "Botanicon Sinicum," pt. 1 *JNCBRAS* 16 (1881); pt.2 *JNCBRAS* 25 (1890-91); pt 3. *JNCBRAS* 29 (1894-5).
79. Florence Ayscough, *Tu Fu: The Autobiography of a Chinee Poet 712-770* (London: Jonathan Cape, 1929) 174.
80. The expression of this interest was to become stronger in the 1930s, largely through the activities of Arthur de Carle Sowerby, a widely published naturalist, NCBRAS President 1935-40, and Director of the Shanghai Museum 1925-46.
81. Ayscough, *Mirror* 72-3.
82. The Yuyuan dragon wall is illustrated in Ayscough, *Mirror*, 233.
83. Ink rubbings were part of the sizeable bequest Ayscough's second husband made to The Art Institute of Chicago in 1943.
84. Ayscough, *Mirror* 94.
85. Recently, for example, pieces from this bequest were displayed in the exhibition "Transcending Tradition: The Flowering of a New Artistic Culture in Shanghai," May 6 to Oct. 29, 2006, The

Art Institute of Chicago.
86. Ayscough, *Mirror* 25.
87. This is much the same configuration as noted by J.G. Ballard the next decade, where sumptuous western villas contained "overly spacious kitchens, room-sized pantries with giant refrigerators, central heating and double glazing, and a bathroom for every bedroom." J.G. Ballard, *Miracles of Life: An Autobiography* (London: Harper Perennial, 2008) 12.
88. MacNair, *Correspondence* 207.
89. MacNair, *Correspondence* 214.
90. Ayscough's correspondence with Amy Lowell after the couple's return from China makes reference to many lecture engagements.
91. Newspaper accounts and society pages made much of this flamboyance. See, for example "Far Eastern Things Touch Our Chicago," *Chicago Daily Tribune* 8 Feb., 1931: H1.
92. I am grateful to Peter Sanger for this piece of information.
93. These are among the Honorary Members listed in the *JNCBRAS* 52 (1921): 237.
94. *The Society of Woman Geographers: A Register of its Records in the Library of Congress* 14 May 2009 http://lcweb2.loc.gov/service/mss/eadxmlmss/eadpdfmss/2005/ms005005.pdf.
95. *The Geographical Journal* 71.1 (January 1928): 111.
96. Sanger 60.
97. *Proceedings of the American Oriental Society* 51.4 (Dec. 1931): 354.
98. *Proceedings of the Royal Anthropological Institute* 62 (Jul.-Dec. 1932): 394.
99. "Far Eastern Things" H1.
100. Harley Farnsworth MacNair, review of *The Autobiography of a Chinese Dog* by Florence Ayscough *The Chinese Recorder* (Feb 1927): 135.
101. Florence Ayscough, *The Autobiography of a Chinese Dog* (Boston: Houghton Mifflin Company, 1926) 38, 41.
102. Ayscough, *Tu Fu*, 158-9.
103. Ayscough, *Tu Fu* 116.
104. *JNCBRAS* 65 (1934): 204.
105. MacNair, *Incomparable Lady* 5.
106. Sanger 67.

107. Sanger 67-8.
108. *JNCBRAS* 66 (1935): xi.
109. "Wedding in Britain for Mrs Ayscough," *The New York Times* 26 Sept. 26 1935: 20.
110. Elinor Pearlstein discusses some of this collection, and includes a photograph of Ayscough and MacNair in "Colour, Life, Moment," *Art Institute of Chicago Museum Studies* 26.2 (2000): 88-9.
111. Sanger argues that these activities should not be understood in a negative sense, as opportunistic forays during a politically tumultuous period, but as actions aimed as securing these artworks for posterity. He points out that these collections were gifted to public institutions after Ayscough's death.
112. *JNCBRAS* 70 (1939): xx.
113. Maurice T. Price, "Harley Farnsworth MacNair (July 22, 1891-June 22, 1947)," *The Far East Quarterly* 8:1 (Nov. 1848): 54.
114. Ayscough and Lowell, *Fir Flower Tablets* 10.

AMY LOWELL
The Fragrance of Adapted Chinese Verse in FIR FLOWER TABLETS
Janet Roberts

"To be introduced to a new and magnificent literature, not through the medium of the usual more or less accurate translation but directly, as one might burrow it out for one's self with the aid of a dictionary, is an exciting and inspiring thing...I hold that it is more important to reproduce the perfume of a poem than its metrical form, as no translation can possibly reproduce both." – Amy Lowell, (1874-1925) preface to Fir-Flower Tablets

In the early part of the twentieth century, we find a transmigration of the fragrance of Chinese poetry into English, in the transliterations of Florence Ayscough and the versifications of Amy Lowell in Fir Flower Tablets. Literary critic, William Schwartz's words witness: *"If we ever graft Far Eastern branches upon the stock of English poetry, we will turn back to Amy Lowell's Oriental verse with the gratitude and respect due to an inspired explorer."* The geopolitical environment in the early 20th century, in which Amy Lowell adapted Florence Asycough's translations, claimed revisionist views of the world, which have relevance in the 21st century.

Scholar, Adrienne Munich, having taken up the rescue, among others, of Amy Lowell from oblivion, asserts: *"These powerfully beautiful translations place Lowell at the forefront of imagist poets who looked to Asia for inspiration, and, together with her adapted Asian forms, constitute a major contribution to modernism."*[1] Amy Lowell was among those writers, Imagists and Modernists, who drew attention to the poetry and art of China and Japan in terms of both interpretation of and in practice of lyrics in the Japanese style, as well as experiments with versification of Chinese poetry in the first part of the 20th century. Revisionist scholarship is restoring Amy Lowell to our cultural memory.

"I, too, am a rare Pattern... I would choose/To lead him

Amy Lowell in the garden at Sevenels. By permission of the Houghton Library, Harvard University. MS Am 62 (1)

in a maze along the patterned paths", says Lowell in her most anthologized poem, "Patterns" (1915) which details the pattern of a woman's dress and her reverie in a stroll in a patterned garden, interrupted by learning of the death of her lover in a war. Walks in her father's extensive gardens, in their 12 acres of land, at Sevenels, in Brookline, Massachusetts, expressed both his and Amy's own love of horticulture. Amy Lowell continued to sustain this love of flowers, evident in "Lilacs", another poem for which she is remembered. Botanicals contextualize Amy Lowell's New England heritage, shared with Emily Dickinson, known at her death, not for her unpublished poetry, but for her beautiful flower garden.

In Lowell's poems, North American flowers are abundant; favorites are "foxglove" and a special predilection for "blue larkspur". Adrienne Munich observes in Amy Lowell's mention of flowers associated with Asia, that is, camellias and peonies, provision of an Asian influence in her poems. "Nostalgia", "Vespers", and "Afterglow" illustrate close affinities between Imagism and Western notions of Chinese poetry. Illustrative are the following: *"Peonies/the strange pink employs "the empty palanquin" floor, where "the plum blossoms constantly increase".*

Fragrance in flowers such as orchids, the plum blossom, the peach, and the peony play a dramatic role in Chinese literature. It is not only the "flower" itself, as a natural item, in its botanical specificity; the poet is concerned with the act of the memory evoked in an image of petals falling, associated with a woman, and the scent which lingers, in her passage. More literally, the source of fragrance is a reaction between the external perfume, made of the essence of flowers – roses, jasmine, camellias – and when a woman wears a "perfume", the oils of which mingle with her skin scent, and will distinguish her, from anyone else. The fragrance is what remains once she leaves the room. Marcel Proust envoked such memoire d'aide of a sensual or sensory experience, in a mosaic of unforgettable characters and memories in Le Temps Retrouve, or Time Regained. Likewise, what remains, – even in a scent, as evocative of the experience, or in anticipation of the experience – is sought in the Chinese poem. In "Hidden Fragrance", Jiang Kui (12th c)...*"I wonder how the cold fragrance, coming from the sparse petals, beyond the bamboo groove, disturbs the wine in my cup."*

Fragrance in a Chinese poem as in Chinese tea tasting plays a nuanced role, as in life's composition. Song dynasty poetry composed in Suzhou classical gardens often includes a "Fragrance pavilion". The Blue Wave or Surging Wave garden in Suzhou is such an example. The flowers – orchids, plum, peach, osmanthus – in season – are celebrated not only in viewing their budding and blossoming, in transient beauty, like moments mirrored or captured in poems, but in their "fragrance" that lingers in memory. Such reverie is what remains, after the experience of the floral scenting of the air of the garden, which leaves its imprint in poetry, in calligraphy and painting. However, not only in China, but in England, Vita de Sackville West planted whole gardens based not only on designs of color, but on fragrance, about which she had cultivated a knowledge in Persian gardens.

The perfume of a poem, which Amy Lowell was seeking,

in her adaptations was an "essence" that had given rise to the poem, itself. 2 Concerned with the human heart and the spirit of the piece, as well as with its literal "carriers" of meaning, Lowell sought to mine the feelings in the aftermath of an experience. The subtle suggestive economy of the Chinese poems suited what the Imagists had searched, for, in Pound's words, "no superfluous word". This meta-language is embedded or encoded in the surface language of translation, and the interiority is part of the translation of a prosaic experience into a poetic essence. Access to the soul made visible in language manifests for those courageous enough not to follow pedestrian routes, but to make poetry of their lives. Such was the choice of Amy Lowell, as she approached her 30's.

Amy Lowell, was, first and foremost, a poet, a player with language, with pattern, with strategies and schematics to maximize, with the greatest economy, and precision, the human language to express feelings. She did not know Chinese. She was a translator of French poetry, so that experience prepared her for the chance she had, to work with an old friend from adolescence, or Florence Wheelock Asycough, a resident in Shanghai, a librarian for the Royal Asiatic Society who occupied herself with translations of classical poems.[2]

Amy Lowell did not travel to China, but spent most of her life in her native New England. Like Emily Dickinson of Amherst, she would remain in her father's house, her childhood family home, and create a world of music, drama, poetry and art. She purchased the family home Sevenals, in Brookline, Massachusetts, a suburb of Boston, (also a home to the poet Anne Sexton) from her brothers. One brother, Percival, was to become a famous astronomer, who discovered the planet, Pluto, and created the Lowell Observatory in Arizona, and the other, Abbott Lawrence Lowell, was president of Harvard University. Both of her parents died by the time she was 26. Lowell also kept the second home, in Dublin, a retreat into the mountains of New Hampshire.

Born on February 9 in 1874, Amy Lowell lived to be

51 years old, and died in May, 1925. Three volumes of poetry were published after her death. Most notably, *What's O'Clock* (1926) achieved, posthumously, for her, the Pulitzer Prize in poetry. Starting to write at the age of 28, Amy wrote six volumes of poetry, two volumes of criticism, and a two–volume biography of John Keats, and innumerable reviews and articles. A best selling author, her books usually went into 2 or 3 printings and were sold out in advance publication. The prodigious, prolific, and prophetic poet, Amy Lowell, graduated from private schools in Boston at age 17 and continued her self cultivation and further education, tutored in her father's library, and in the bookstacks of the Boston Atheneum, which her great-grandfather John Lowell III had founded. She was well known for her dramatic performative poetry readings. Damon's biography provides account of her reading for the benefit of the MacDowell Colony, dining at the Cosmopolitan Club in Manhattan, reading at the Morgan Library, and of being constantly on tour, providing sold out lectures in cities across America.

Harriet Munroe, Editor of POETRY, Chicago, said of Amy Lowell's dominance in American Letters, " *The force which Miss Lowell's New England ancestors put into founding and running cotton mills... she put into conquering an art and making it express and serve her.*" Amy Lowell's independent wealth was inherited from her father's textile mills. As Virginia Woolf proposed, in A Room of One's Own, to write, one needs a room of one's own, and Amy Lowell had the prerequisites, even a house of her own, and like her European counterpart, servants aplenty, including women companions, to enable her to pursue her writing and chosen career as a poet. Lowell never married, an early engagement having been broken, by the young man, in part, due to her overweight, bordering, on obesity, which even a starvation cruise on the Nile could not remedy. The famous poem "Pattern" touches upon this loss of her fiancé.

Amy Lowell was, in some ways, a nationalist in her poetry aspirations, as was Mary Anne Moore, in that they did not want to rely on Europe, but America, for their subject matter. Lowell would say that the New Poetry was blazing a trail toward Nationalism far *"more subtle and intense than any settlement houses and waving the American flag in schools can ever achieve."*Transporting herself from the Victorian era in America, into the Roaring Twenties, Amy Lowell, was part of formulating a New Poetry, for a country shedding the constraints of European inheritance and finding its own voice. In a post Emersonian age, extending beyond the Transcendentalists in Concord, Massachusetts, that is, Thoreau, Emerson, and the outspoken Margaret Fuller.[3] – Amy Lowell read on the platforms of poetry across the country with Robert Frost, a lifelong friend, and Carl Sandburg, who were equally adamant about the new voice of America. She achieved another "first" by recognizing Wallace Stevens, who would be celebrated as a major poet, whereas she was antipathetic to T.S. Eliot and Ezra Pound, again, it seems, on nationalistic grounds.

Orientalism was a place to which the poets turned as distraction from the War. Li Po and Tu Fu's poetry became pivotal to early 20th century Modernism. Contemporary Chinese novelist Xialong Qiu, in his novel, <u>Red Mandarin Dress</u> espouses a similar understanding: *"American Imagist poets were indebted to classical Chinese poetry."*[4]

JAPAN. PICTURES FROM THE FLOATING WORLD.(1919)
Amy wrote: *"A constant stream of pictures, prints, and kakemanos flowed in upon me...which made Japan so vivid to my imagination that I cannot realize that I have never been there".* Amy Lowell's journey into Asian poetry began as a *mental traveler* to Asia, only, first to Japan, through the letters and pictures sent by her older brother, Percy, who went to Japan, shortly after Perry opened trade relations. Percival Lowell (Percy) lived in Japan, and Korea, where he served as foreign secretary and consul from 1895, the year of Amy's birth to 1916, when she was 21 He wrote four books on the Far East, including *"The Soul of the Far East"* and *"Occult Japan".*

Amy Lowell grew increasingly interested in Japan, naturally as Boston was a center for study of Far Eastern

Art, along with the collections at Harvard University, in Cambridge, which are now in the Sackler collection of Asian Art, and the Isabelle Gardner house museum in Boston. Japanese guests were often in the Lowell home, visiting her brother, Abbot Lawrence Lowell, then president of Harvard. Quintessentially, Amy Lowell "grew up" in a world of Japanese allusion, through her brother's letters, which left a strong impression in her early years, and would influence her poetry to the extent of her creating a whole volume,"Pictures from the Floating World" (1919) centered on her love of Japanese poetry and art, as well it allowed her to write poems in the Japanese style.[5]

Amy Lowell's friendship with the great art collector Isabelle Gardner fueled what was to become a passionate pursuit of Asian art forms. Japanese art historian and critic Okakura Kakuzo (author of The Book of Tea) influenced Gardener in her travelling to Asia, and in her collecting and rearrangement of the museum to give Asian art a greater role. Kakuzo helped Gardner to arrange an exhibition devoted to Japanese culture and performed the tea ceremony at her Museum.[6]

Sharing a passion for woodblock prints with the French Impressionist painter, Claude Monet, and the American Impressionist painter, James Whistler – whose paintings she had purchased – Amy Lowell chose *"A coloured print by Shokei" and "A Japanese Wood-Carving"* inspired by woodblock prints, for inclusion in her first book, *A Dome of Many Coloured Glass* (1912). Amy Lowell's familiarity with the Japanese haiku form further stimulated innovation found in her poems, " Lacquer Prints" published in her fifth volume of poetry, *Pictures from a Floating World* in 1919. This poem illustrates Lowell's fulfillment of her intention:

Nuance.
Even the iris bends //When a butterfly lights upon it.
– September 1919

The haiku had now become a continuous thread in the fabric of her poetry. A suite of *"Twenty Four Hokku on a*

Modern Theme", and "Anniversary" appear in *Poetry* June 1921 and were later incorporated into "What's O'Clock" (1925) which, posthumously, won her the Pulitzer prize.

"The adoption of a foreign form of verse surely marks a deeper, more vital influence than the mere poetical interpretation of an eastern work of art ..." was the astute observation of literary critic, Richard Benvenuto.[7] The reticence, economy, and suggestiveness that Lowell found in Japanese haiku reinforced Imagist principles imitating musical sounds. It is also possible, as Margaret Gibson, contemporary poet, explores. to adopt the subject matter of Japanese art, in free verse. [8]

It is appropriate to recall that Ezra Pound's two most famous lines, "*A Station in the Metro*", "*The apparition of these faces in a crowd; Petals on a wet, black bough*"... emerged from the influence of Japanese haiku. The emphasis in much Oriental poetry, on objectivity, subtle suggestiveness, and precise language gave Lowell a new forum in which to write about her own inmost feelings with less attachment.[9]

Pictures from a Floating World also contains seven '*Chinoiseries*' "written in a quasi-Oriental idiom", but with allusions to Japanese lacquerware and screens, which were later incorporated into FIR FLOWER TABLETS. 1921.[10]

The trade with Japan and the China Trade were a part of Amy Lowell's New England heritage. Early on, Lowell celebrates this tea, porcelain and silk trade era in lines such as : "*I might be sighting a tea-clipper,/ Tacking into the blue bay,/ Just back from Canton/ With her hold full of green and blue porcelain....* or in "The Red Lacquer Music Stand", where she writes... "*A music-stand of crimson lacquer, long since brought/In some fast clipper-ship from China, quaintly wrought...*" and in "*Lilacs*"... *When a ship was in from China/You called to them: "Goose-quill men, goose-quill men, May is a month for flitting.*"

Like fragrance in Chinese verse, many Chinese poets write the words "to a tune", or mention a musical instrument. Amy Lowell was serious about music, about music transmitted and transformed into poetry, and certainly she was concerned, in Fir Flower Tablets, about rhythms. She put into words, the effect of listening to Igor Stravinsky's "Grotesques" for string quartet.

Lowell asked a composer,[11] Charles Martin Loeffler (1861-1935) a mutual friend of the great art collector, Isabelle Gardner[12] to give Lowell pictures, or "images" in music, for which she could find the words. Loeffler had already set music for the French poems of Verlaine and Baudelaire. Amy Lowell here was following Ruskin's dictum, that all the arts aspire to Music, and fulfilling what intellectual passion she had for music, shared with Carl Engle, a French composer, a part of their circle. At Sevenels, Lowell presented private concerts of French music, including Claude Debussy and Erik Satie.

Given Amy Lowell's love of music, her effort to translate music into her poems, in her words, *"reproduce the effect of the music in another medium"*. She qualifies her use of rhythm: *"I wanted to try something more, something less obvious than mere rhythm, and closer to the essence of musical speech."* True to being an Imagist, in reproducing sounds, Lowell discovered essential images and ideas in music, and made allusions, to music, in her poems, but most significantly tried to translate the instrument and music into language.[13] Musicologist, Ambrose says of Lowell's approach: *"...like a sensitive translator,(Lowell) treats the original with a care and respect that can only issue from knowledge and understanding".* Thomas Hardy had commented to her that he found her efforts in making music, poetry, successful.[14]

Lowell was attuned to the Modernist synthesis of painting and music arising out of images in poetry.[15] *"Poetry is as much an art to be heard as is music,"* Lowell was to assert, accounting for the necessary performative quality in the poet, for which she was well known. In her polyphonic verse, Lowell uses musical analogy and musical techniques, as visual experiences to shape images, illustrating how brilliantly one art can illuminate another. In a letter to Florence Asycough, Amy reports that a friend, John Alden Carpenter, would like to have some of her own poems set to music.

When the composer and violinist Charles Loeffler invited Lowell to his own home, in Medford, his playing of the d'Indy violin sonata in his music room inspired Lowell to conflate Chinese imagery and musical notation, in the last lines of her poem :

The brown Chinese junks sail silently / Around the brown walls.
A cricket hurried across the bare floor.The windows are black for the sun has set.
Only the candles,Clustered like altar lamps on their tall candlestick, /
Light the violinist as he plays.

Here we see a commingling of western and eastern images in Lowell, or Chinese poetry with western aspects. The Chinese influence was relatively weaker than Japanese verse, as she was less often moved to composition, in the Chinese manner , such as in "Wind and Silver" in "What's O'Clock".[16]

In her own translations of rhythms in FIR FLOWER TABLETS, Miss Lowell stated in her preface that she had *"as a rule, strictly adhered to the lines of the original stanza,"* and poetic license was exercised *"solely in the interest of cadence."* In contrast, Ezra Pound is known for shouting, "Break the line, break the line!" [17]

Refashioning the poems in English, first required knowledge of the laws of Chinese versification, but then Amy Lowell says she had to respect the technical limits but found it impossible to follow either the rhythms or rhyme schemes of the originals as she had no experience of the spoken language. One wonders if during their sessions if Florence did not recite the poems in the original Chinese. However, since Amy did not hear the idiom of Chinese speakers, and did not step foot on Chinese soil, it is no wonder, that given she worked with the English transliterations, she could hardly exactly replicate the original rhythms.

I have chosen this particular poem, "On Hearing the Buddhist Priest of Shu Play His Table Lute" with its subject of music, of playing music, and of Lowell's effort to convey music in language, and its burden of allusion, to contrast it with the more "direct" and straightforward translation of Bynner. David Hinton, the only translator to know Chinese, shows how far the art of translation has come, in terms of reproducing the idiom.

On Hearing the Buddhist Priest
Of Shu Play His Table-Lute Li Tai'Po

The Priest of the Province of Shu, carrying his table-lute in
a cover of green, shot silk,
Comes down the Western slope of the peak of Mount Omei.
He moves his hands for me, striking the lute.
It is like listening to the water in ten thousand ravines, and
the
Wind in ten thousand pine trees.
The traveller's heart is washed clean as in flowing water.
The echoes of the overtones join with the evening bell.
I am not conscious of the sunset behind the jade- grey hill,
Nor how many and dark are the Autumn clouds.

– Amy Lowell, Fir Flower Tablets, December 1921.

On Hearing Chun. The Buddhist
Monk from Shu play his Lute.

The monk from Shu with his green silk lute case,
Walking west down O-Mei Mountain,
Has brought me by one touch of the strings,
The breath of pines in a thousand valleys.
I hear him in the cleansing brook,
I hear him in the icy bells;
And I feel no change though the mountain darkens
And cloudy autumn heaps the sky.

–Witter Bynner, Jade Mountain.

David Hinton's translation, Burton Watson praises, "Hinton's translations, while remaining faithful to the meaning and spirit of the original, are consistently imaginative in language and effective as English poetry, and he has shown a remarkable skill in capturing the style and voice of the different poets he has tackled."

An earlier critic, Burton Schwartz was not so generous to Amy Lowell and Florence Asycough. "One *regrets especially that Fir-Flower Tablets do not give a better idea of Chinese poetic form.*"[18] One wonders how much Schwartz knew of Chinese "form".

Carrying a ch'in cased in green silk, a monk Descended from O-mei Mountain in the west. Li ta-po
When he plays, even in a few first notes,
I hear the pines of ten thousand valleys,
And streams rinse my wanderer's heart clean.
Echoes linger among temple frost-fall bells
Night coming unnoticed in emerald mountains,
Autumn clouds banked up, gone dark and deep.
　　　　　　　　　　　　　　–David Hinton(1996) [19]

But let's turn the pages of history back to that fateful moment when Amy Lowell heard of Imagism and went to London to meet Ezra Pound(1895-1972) in 1913, where Pound was pouring over Fenollossa's *notes* and extrapolating notes on Chinese poetry. Ernest Francisco Fenollosa died in 1908 – leaving his manuscripts and notes to his literary executor, Ezra Pound. Earlier, Pound had included several paraphrases from the Chinese in *Des Imagistes* (April 1914), in which he would publish Amy Lowell's poem, "In a Garden", along with his poetry and that of HD(Hilda Doolittle), Richard Aldington, and William Carlos Williams.

Pound subsequently published Fenollosa's essay on "The Chinese Written Character" and his conception of the ideogram in *The Little Review* (1918). Amy Lowell, intrigued by the Chinese classical poems, was inspired by what she saw that Pound was able to achieve, without knowing Chinese language. She praised Pound's publication of *Cathay (*1915) in a letter to Harriet Munroe, editor of POETRY in Chicago. The discovery of classical Chinese poetry proved a decisive moment for Lowell, as it had, for Pound.

It is only when Lowell returned to America and wanted to democratize or widen the spread of the Imagist movement – which focused on "an intellectual and emotional instant of time" – rather than maintain its exclusivity, that Pound and she parted ways and even grew antagonistic. Pound would argue, *"There is no democracy in the arts".* Lowell believed in a verse, American, and modern...and shared with her contemporary Robert Frost – an egalitarian view towards readership, that as she would say, *"anyone with a spark of poetry in them, be they blacksmiths or millionaires"* could find pleasure in poetry. Pound disparaged Lowell, calling her version of the movement, "Amygysm"...betraying a fear of *"spawning inferior American women poets in a literary democracy of equal suffrage"*...

Undauntable, Amy Lowell, during the first World War, was to edit and publish three Imagist anthologies under the title, "Some Imagist Poets" Boston: Houghton Mifflin, 1915-17. Only Ezra Pound and Amy Lowell were published poets. Pound refused publication, and subsequently he and Wyndham Lewis would turn to Vorticism.[20] Only Ezra Pound and Witter Bynner went to Japan and China.[21]

Both novelists and poets, Thomas Hardy and D.H. Lawrence were lifelong friends and gave encouragement to Amy Lowell in her projects. As Thomas Hardy had admired her music in poetry, D.H. Lawrence wrote "Women In Love" on a typewriter Lowell gave him, and wrote to her, October 9, 1921, from Sicily, *"My dear Amy... Have you done your Chinese book? I shall be interested in that."* Both men encouraged her projects. Reciprocally, Amy reciprocally published and promoted Lawrence's novels in America.[22]

Amy Lowell was off and running, setting herself immediately to work, as she formerly had with Imagist poetry, with Pound as her exemplar. She wrote about her own translation project, (August 16, 1918),*"I do not claim that these translations are any better as poems, nor perhaps as good as Ezra's but much more accurate".* These are the "re-creations" with mixed success, which she versified at the request of Florence Asycough, for the exhibition of "wall pictures" at an exposition. Amy Lowell had an authoritative voice in poetry, as one of the leading poets of the day. The first of Amy Lowell's versions of Chinese poetry appear in "*Chinese Written Wall Pictures*", Poetry, February, 1919, the same year her volume of Japanese inspired poetry, appears, and are incorporated in *Fir Flower Tablets in* Dec. 1921.

To provide historical perspective, in 1852, the era of Queen Victoria, the year before Admiral Perry's great expeditions to Japan and the Far East, Richard Henry Stoddard included some Chinese subjects in his Poems and Chivers published his "Chinese Serenade" . (P. 586 Damon) Though now considered archaic, Herbert A. Giles, for many years H.B.M Consul at Ningbo, and later professor of Chinese at Cambridge, published English verse translations of the poetry of China as early as 1898; his famous History of Chinese Literature came out in 1901. So early ground was broken, by these pioneering efforts and Florence Asycough and Amy Lowell would follow, leaving more quiet footsteps.

A CHINESE FLAVOR

A flavor, in its aftertaste, is rather like a perfume's scent. Amy Lowell writes to Asycough emphasizing a preference for retaining the flavor of the originals[22] and in her preface to Fir Flower Tablets expresses admiration for Waley's which do retain this flavor of the original Chinese [23]

When French critic, Jean Catel reviewed *Fir Flower Tablets* in Le Mercure de France(1926), he praised the accuracy and flavor of the English renderings of Chinese poems. However, after reading the the McNair publication of the letters between Ayscough and Lowell, Catel recants, "*Chinese poetry was to her(Amy Lowell) the most delicate of dishes, her collaborating with Florence Ayscough a means of justifying her approach to it. ... The oriental flavor has evaporated under the touch, however, delicate, of a Western hand.*"

Lowell's appreciation and enthusiasm for the Chinese flavor in poetry and poets appears in a letter to Florence

Ayscough, August 16, 1919:

The great poets of the T'ang Dynasty, particularily Li T'ai Po, are without doubt among the finest poets that the world has ever had. .. He seems to me to rank second to none in any country in lyric poetry, and it seems to me as though Du Fu were equally fine.....

As for Tu Fu, about whom she would write a praiseworthy biography, Ayscough would concur with Arthur Waley that because of the difficulty of translation – they will include only his simpler poems.

One of the most discussed poems from both translators, Waley and Asycough/Lowell is "Drinking under Moonlight' but another of the most cited poems, is a poem taught in primary school in China, and is still familiar to any Chinese reader. It is useful to recall that Li Po is famous for falling into the river, drowning, not while looking at his own reflection like Narcissus in the Greek myth, but while trying to embrace the reflection of the moon.

"Night Thoughts" by Li Po (AD712-760) High Tang period
In front of my bed the moonlight is very bright,
I wonder if that can be frost on the floor?
I lift up my head and look full at the full moon, the dazzling moon.
I drop my head and think of the home of old days.
–Amy Lowell, Fir Flower Tablets, 1921

When subjected to the scrutiny of Chinese readers, college teachers, "lifting up" and "looking full" at the "full moon", and the "dazzling moon" were not considered accurate in phrasing or in the choice of adjectives. Likewise, "the home of old days" emphasizes past time; what the poet is missing is his home. In contrast, David Hinton's version captures the natural idiom and met with immediate praise from the same Chinese audience:

Thoughts in Night Quiet
Seeing moonlight here at my bed,
And thinking it's frost on the ground,

I look up, gaze at the mountain moon,
Then back, dreaming of my old home.
　　–David Hinton, The Selected Poems of Li Po, 1996.

Bird and flower imagery play a supporting role in Lowell's poetry, demonstrating a transtextual and cross cultural linkage with the bird and flower imagery of traditional Chinese poetry and painting. Along with admiration of the flowers in her extensive gardens, Amy Lowell enjoyed the singing of birds. Birdsong is common in Lowell's own poetry, an affinity shared by many poets. Lowell's admiration for and study of the Romantic poet, John Keats, whose biography she made her life long project, affords another example, in that Keat's most famous poem – along with his unrequited lovers sealed in embrace on the Grecian urn – is about the song of the Nightingale. Let's look at a version by Lowell and by Waley to see the relationship between their versions of the poem about listening to an oriole's morning song.

Po Chu-I.
"Hearing the Early Oriole (Written in Exile)"

The sun rose while I slept. I had not yet risen
When I heard an early oriole above the roof of my house.
Suddenly it was like the Royal Park at dawn,
With birds calling from the branches of the ten-thousand-year trees.
I thought of my time as a Court Official
When I was meticulous with my pencil in the Audience Hall.
At the height of Spring, in occasional moments of leisure,
I would look at the grass and growing things,
And at dawn and at dusk I would hear this sound.
Where do I hear it now?
In the lonely solitude of the City of Hsun Yang.
The bird's song is certainly the same,
The change is in the emotions of the man.
If I could only stop thinking that I am at the ends of the earth,

I wonder, would it be so different from the Palace after all?

Amy Lowell, Fir Flower Tablets

Then, we turn, in contrast to Arthur Waley's version:
Po-Chu-I "Hearing the Early Oriole"
When the sun rose, I was still lying in bed;
An early oriole sang, on the roof of my house.
For a moment, I thought of the Regent park at dawn.
When the Birds of Spring greeted their Lord from his trees.
I remembered the days when I served before the throne
Pencil, in hand, on duty at the Ch'eng-ming;
At the height of Spring, when I paused an instant from work,
Morning and evening, was this the voice I heard:
Now in my exile the oriole sings again
In the dreary stillness of Hsun yang town...
The bird's note cannot really have changed;
All the difference lies in the listener's heart.
If he could but forget that he lives at the world's end,
The bird would sing as it sang in the Palace of old.

–Arthur Waley.

FIR FLOWER TABLETS (1921): A PATHWAY TO A NEW WORLD

Florence Asycough, was born in China and spent most of her adult life residing in China, so like Pearl S. Buck, she grew up, exposed to a second language in a bi-lingual environment. She collaborated with a Chinese professor, Nung Chu, in her occupation with translations, and then invited her childhood friend, Amy Lowell, now a well known poet, to adapt the poems into English. Both women admired Arthur Waley's translations, appearing in periodicals when they started their collaboration. Arthur Waley's translations *One Hundred and Seventy Chinese Poems* had appeared in (1918)[25]. He was considered to better able to get the meter of the poems, right, having insight into the euphonic and tonal qualities of Chinese. He had taught himself Japanese and Chinese, as overseer of the Asian

Amy Lowell at the age when she met Florence Asycough. By permission of the Houghton Library, Harvard University. MS Am 62 (1).

collections at the British Museum.

Lowell would state, *"Mrs. Ayscough has been to me the pathway to a new world. No one could be a more sympathetic go between for a poet and his translator,... (from the Preface to Fir Flower Tablets" pp vi-vii)* The two women are considered to have enjoyed a happy collaboration, primarily accomplished by lengthy professional correspondence, exchanged by transatlantic letters for nearly a decade, from 1917 until Miss Lowells' death in 1925. Since neither professed to have the other's skills – Asycough was not a poet, and Lowell, not a sinologist – their association was a "continually augmenting pleasure". (Lowell, preface)

The Chinese collaborator with Florence Asycough would say of Amy Lowell's poem adaptations, "the writing brush of Madame Asycough's friend (Amy Lowell) is full of life's movement". Ayscough replied, *"That you see is what Heaven does. Anyone with patience and your help, could do my part but hers (Lowell's) is a gift from heaven."*

In 1917, Amy Lowell was invited by Florence Wheelock Asycough(1875-1942), during one of her customary visits, to America, to shape into poetry, her transliterations of Chinese poems , which would accompany the exhibition of Florence's own collection of Chinese paintings, now at the Art Museum in Chicago 35 Lowell grew enthusiastic about the reading of Chinese poetry and about a translation project with her old childhood friend. It was when she was 15 that she met Florence, age 11 at Miss Quincey's School, as her father retired from China in 1889. Their 30 year friendship would bear fruit, in the collaboration over four years of correspondence between Boston and Shanghai, in the wartime mails.

(from the Preface to Fir Flower Tablets" pp vi-vii)

Among these paintings were a number of examples of "the Written Pictures". Among these (Ayscough) had made some rough translations which she intended to use to illustrate her lectures. She brought them to me with the request that I put them into poetic shape. I was fascinated by the poems, and, as we talked them over, we realized that here was a field in which we should like to work. When she returned to China, it was agreed that we should make a volume of translations from the classic Chinese writers. Such translations were in the line of her usual work, and I was anxious to read the Chinese poets as nearly in the original as it was possible for me to do. At first, we hardly considered publication. But an enthusiastic publisher kept before us our ultimate goal."

Amy Lowell was not the translator, or carrier of meanings, but the adapter, or re-maker of the poems in the target language, English. She may have produced more of a grafting of form, than an intrinsic new form, or even a hybrid. *"To be introduced to a new and magnificent literature, not through the medium of the usual more or less accurate translation but directly, as one might burrow it out for one's self with the aid of a dictionary, is an exciting and inspiring thing..."* Lowell acknowledges that the study of Chinese, as well as the study of poetry, require lifelong learning, and clarifies that she has not taken up the Chinese language or the field of sinology, as had the translator of the poems, Florence Asycough.

Lowell defended their method, though she seems to balk at all the allusions, by her use of the descriptor, "copious", and reference to the fact that Florence "deemed her to know" all this contextual material... *" I had in fact, four different means of approach to a poem. The Chinese text, for rhyme-scheme and rhythm: the dictionary meanings of the words; the analyses of the characters; and , for the fourth, a careful paraphrase by Mrs. Ayscough, to which she added copious notes to acquaint me with all the allusions, historical, mythological, geographical and technical, that she deemed it necessary for me to know. and let me state at the outset that I know no Chinese" (page x)* – Amy Lowell (1922).

Asycough would cater to the literal and Lowell, to the literary form of the poem. Ayscough is adamant about idiom, or the way the language is spoken, as she lived in China, hearing the language, rather than metrics, the way the line is written to convey sound and meaning.[27] One wonders if Ayscough did not read the poems in Chinese, during their conferences, so Lowell would have some sense of the euphonics in Chinese.

Amy Lowell, explicated the method employed with Florence Asycough, which was to separate a Chinese character into its components. Amy Lowell writes – giving evidence of detecting the importance of the radical in the Chinese character – which is credited to her knowledge of Pound's translation of Fenollosa – in a letter to Harriet Munroe, editor of the prestigious POETRY magazine, in Chicago, from Brookline, Massachusetts, 19, June, 1918:

"...I have made a discovery...which, I think, must be well

known in Chinese literature; namely, that the roots of the character are the things which give the poetry its overtones, taking the place of adjectives and imaginary writing...One cannot translate a poem into anything like the proper spirit, taking the character meaning alone. It is necessary in every case to go the root of a character, and that will give the key to why that particular word is used and not some other which means the same thing when exactly translated. Mrs. Ayscough quite agrees with me in this. This is the key to the situation, and it is the hunting of these roots that she is doing."[28]

In The Journal of the North China RAS (Royal Asiatic Society Journal) Vol 1. 1919) a skeptical reviewer, who signs M., expresses doubts: "... In many ways Mrs. Ayscough is a pioneer, and this idea of hers to extract all she can, and more than others thought they should, may be justified in the end. The character invites such a method as the one suggested...Of course the Chinese protests vigorously against such a treatment. Itself being under rigid rules ,and governed by inexorable laws it seems to object at every port at the idea often being carried too many feet, or being left as short measure. At present we are neutral and stand by to wait and see."

Ayscough[29] justified her notations, which create a heavily annotated edition, and at times, it is thought encumbered the poems. Lowell would work, line by line, with the original translation sent by Asycough, Translators seek the exact word, in the target language, to represent the sense. Oftentimes, Lowell chose a word from Asycough's options and would say, "I think it extremely important not to do any embroidery that the characters do not justify." Strictly adhering to the lines which Ayscough set, "only "cadence" dictated any variance. Lowell cites one instance of changing an "adjective" because there was no equivalent for an architectural term in English. The versions would pass back and forth across the Atlantic, by mail, and ship, during wartime, and finally be reviewed in person at Sevenels. The two women worked hard, to "get it right".[30]

Working together at Sevenals, determined to publish

FIR FLOWER TABLETS, before Witter Bynner's JADE MOUNTAIN, Lowell read poems to visitor, Jessie Rittenhouse – "it was almost as though she(Lowell) herself had written these antique poems." Another time, Florence arrived at Sevenels, for a couple of weeks, in September, during which they did 250 poems by Tu Fu...Mrs. Ayscough went away, and when she returned, they did more Tu Fu poems; and after a party where Mrs Ayscough showed colored lantern slides of Chinese gardens and the Yangtze in the music room, they finished the 500th poem at 4:00AM, October 10. They ran through the 500, to select 200 for their book. The book was finished, but not in time for Christmas.[31] When published, the critics felt, FIR FLOWER TABLETS did not match the quality of her other verse, and it was thought by the author, herself, to perhaps be a "professional mistake".[32]

In January, Bynner who was now president of the Poetry Society,(1922-24) invited a Chinese Scholar, Chan Peng-chun, as the principal speaker who contrasted American and Chinese attitudes towards poetry, which Lowell found very interesting. After Carl Sandburg read "Windy City" at midnight, Lowell finally read, her poem, "Lilacs" at 1:00 AM, when everyone rose in tribute to her. This excerpt says what was important to Amy Lowell, as an American New Poetry was to Walt Whitman, Robert Frost and Carl Sandburg in this time period.

> Heart-leaves of lilac all over New England,
> Roots of lilac under all the soil of New England,
> Lilacs in me because I am New England,
> Because my roots are in it,
> Because my leaves are of it,
> Because my flowers are for it,
> Because it is my country
> And I speak to it of itself
> And sing of it with my own voice
> Since certainly it is mine.

She had not chosen an adaptation of a translation from Fir Flower Tablets.

LE LIVRE DE JADE.

Given Lowell's love of French poetry, it is really conceivable that she read Judith Gautier's "Le Livre de Jade", published one decade, before Fir Flower Tablets. There are certainly parallels to be drawn between the two women. In August, Lowell would write, *"I am absolutely drowned in Chinese literature, all I can get in English and French translations. I am beginning to understand a good many things that I did not understand before... The French translations are on the whole better than the English, but even they have not the peculiar flavor of the originals." (Correspondence, Preface)*

For over half a century in the European literary world, Le Livre de Jade, which Kenneth Rexroth described as "that minor classic of French letters" served – directly and indirectly – as the general French reader's primary access to Chinese poetry. for over a decade in the European literary world. [33] Kenneth Rexroth had listed *"Fir-Flower Tablets"* as *"Very good"*, from the bibliography to his lecture "The Poetry of the Far East in a General Education".

The Symbolist and literary critic, Remy de Gourmont, observed that China was Gautier's passion and "inspired her most beautiful books". In 1867, her volume of 71 Chinese poems had been published under the pseudonym Judith Walter, and was dedicated to her tutor, "Tin –Tun-ling, Chinese Poet". Gautier's father's most significant contribution to shaping his daughter's translation activities occurred in 1863, when he engaged Ding Duling (1830-86), a Chinese as a tutor. His patron, Joseph Marie Calley (1810-62), dispatched to Macau as a missionary to work on a French Chinese dictionary, had passed away. Judith, a diligent pupil, of Chinese, as Florence Asycough would prove to be, had hardly begun to "stammer Chinese" when she undertook the "most difficult and impossible task, which disheartened the most knowledgeable sinologists – that of translating the untranslatable Chinese poets..." [34]

Gautier, at age 20 is more liberal in her translation method. She retitles all the poems and as far as faithfulness to people and places, employs generic terms. As for "breaking the line", she sometimes alternated the order of lines, or omitted them entirely. Where no corollary for the poem in the Chinese can be found, Gautier, or her tutor may have written the poem, implying, again, an ever thin line between translation and adaptation. As for the trans-textual adaptation from the original "rough" versions, Lowell, likewise often thought more than one word substituted for another, and Lowell, like Gautier, is credited with writing her own version of the poem...at times, which probably proved the more successful. [35]

Amy Lowell found a "perfume", and a new "flavor" in Chinese poetry, and defied the untranslatability of a poem's modality, perhaps, most importantly, Chinese lyricism was absorbed and inspired her own poetry. It is difficult for a poet to adapt translations, as a poet's task is to write in his or her own language. Lowell herself, summed up: *"I have "realized that the poem is not just some sentences. It can be the soul. It can be the part of history; and it also can be the connection between the different cultures or literatures. Poetry and history are the textbooks to the heart of man, and poetry is at once the most intimate and the most enduring."*

Contemporary poet Carolyn Forche said it beautifully: *"In our country (America) especially it is necessary for translators to assimilate the poets' labors and, in many of these poems, to construct a vessel in a new language that might resemble the poem shattered by the translator's art then reassembled to suggest the original, bearing the sensibility of the poem into English, but inevitably, without retaining its original music."*

AFTERWORD

Amy Lowell would leave us with this: " I can only say that they are as near the originals as we could make them, and I hope they may give one quarter of the pleasure to our reader that they have to us in preparing them." What a pleasure to rediscover their creative project in translation, in the context of living in Shanghai in the 21st century, with the revival of the Royal Asiatic Society, that this contribution extended from Florence Ayscough, her childhood friend, as a venture in cultural transmission, as more than a graft on the tree, but one of the branches, along with daring to go deeper into the root structures of intertextuality and intercultural relations.

Notes

1. Amy Lowell, New American Poet by Adrienne Munch. P. xxxii in Selected Poems of Amy Lowell. Ed. Adrienne Munch and Melissa Bradshaw. Rutgers University Press, New Brunswick,. NJ USA.
2. Kennedy, George A. Yale Literary Magazine, Vol 126. No. 5. December, 1958. Pp. 24-36. Ernest Fenollosa, "Ezra Pound and the Chinese Character". "the ladies believed that the choice was determined according to how well the *"descriptive allusion"* or the *"undercurrent of meaning"* would enrich the "perfume" of the poem' (p.9) Professor William Hung believes the choice is based on sound values. Kennedy maintains that *"the assembling of twenty characters, however strong their perfume, does not make a Chinese poem"*. Kennedy continues: *"The assumption of the "etymological" translators – Fenollosa, Pound, Ayscough, Lowell, and others – is that the meaning, connotation, allusion, perfume, concreteness of a given Chinese character has remained immutable from pre-historic times."* Kennedy maintains that to translate 8th c poetry, you need to know 8th c language. Kennedy asks a question about Pound, which is the one I answer, about Lowell. *"Does the superiority of Pound's Translation lie in the end-product, the superior style and poetic quality of his English, or does it lie at the source, a deeper penetration into the mind and art of the Chinese poet who furnishes the raw material for the translation?"* He continues. *"Only in rare combination can philologists double as poets, or poets as philologists. The philologist is concerned with excavating expression from a foreign language, the poet with perfecting expression in his own language."* He concludes that Pound is a poet, not a translator.
3. R.W. Emerson and H.D. Thoreau (1817-62) both studied Classics at Harvard, including Chinese Classical thought. Emerson emphasized the "transparent eye" or insight, rather than blind following of tradition (See Frederic Ives Carpenter *Emerson and Asia* (Cambridge Harvard University Press, 1930) and the more recent Arthur Verslius, *American Transcendentalism and Asian Religions* (New York: Oxford University Press) *Walden*

by HD Thoreau includes many allusions to Chinese Confucian thought.
4. Xiaolong Qiu. RED MANDARIN DRESS. NY: St Martin's Press, 2007. Qiu Xialolong, RED MANDARIN DRESS. NY: St. Martin's Press. 2007. *"Shen had been a poet in the forties, writing in a then-fashionable Imagist style. After 1949, he was assigned a job at the Shanghai Museum, where he denounced his earlier poetry as decadent and threw himself into the study of ancient Chinese clothing...." Chapter 7. p 52. As an executive member of the Writers's Association, Chen took it upon himself to arrange for a reprint of Shen's collection....the collection came out and was caught up in the city's collective nostalgia. People were pleased to rediscover a poetic witness of those golden years before the revolution. A young critic pointed out that the American Imagist poets were indebted to classical Chinese poetry and that Shen, labeled an Imagist, was actually restoring the ancient tradition. The article appealed to a group of "new nationalist" and the collection sold fairly well" p53"So it's like classical Chinese poetry, Chen cut in "Imagination rises out of what the poet does not say, or not directly...You are still so good with your Imagist touch, Master Shen...". p. 62* This was brought to my attention, as relevant, by Fiona Lindsay Shen.PhD. Art History.
5. Bradshaw, Melissa and Munich, Adrienne, Editors. Amy Lowell, American Modern. Rutgers University Press, New Brunswick, NJ 2004.... Andrew Thacker starts a revisionism in creating an Amy Lowell canon..." He compares Lowell's polyphonic practice and Mikhail Bakhtin's notion of polyphony in the revolutionary aesthetics of Russian novelists while drawing upon modernist synthesis to show how it forms an aesthetic of music and painting in Lowell"s prose poetry
6. *Journeys East,* an exhibition held at the Isabelle Gardner museum in Boston, in Spring, 2009, considered the complex interaction of travel, collecting and museum formation in Isabella Gardner's continuing dialogue with Asia. In the exhibition, Gardner's travel albums and Asian objects included Japanese screens, a monumental bronze Buddha, along with Indian jewelry and Chinese snuff bottles.
7. Benvenuto, Richard. AMY LOWELL. Michigan State University, Twayne, Boston, 1985. Chapter Six. Imagists and Impressionists:

The Life Of Amy Lowell. The Major Lyrics p. 120
8. Schwartz, p. 149.
9. *Autumn Grasses*, LSU (Louisiana State University Press). English-based free verse filled with the spirit of Zen. And another example is: "Sculptress, Johanna Dellenbaugh, A Year in Haiku". Preface, "Haiku: Quickening the Mind's Eye" by Janet Roberts. Beechgate Productions. NJ. 2005.http://www.beechgate.com
10. Asycough's husband, Harley Farnsworth McNair criticizes the title, "Chinoiseries", as gold screens are Japanese, and other objects were Korean, not Chinese....implying Lowell's conflation of things Asian, under the rubric of "chinoiserie", with what was known, that is, Japan. Earlier poets had been attracted by surface flair or "decorative" elements, such as those adapted in patterns of china, wallpaper and draperies, into Western design, in their verse. There is a question as to whether Lowell was seeking more than surfaces, which her participation in Modernism, would imply in its eschewal of sentiment.
11. Ambrose. Lowell to Loeffler, 24 September 1918 and 7 October 1919. Lowell Collection. Houghton Library, Harvard University, Cambridge.
12. Ambrose, Jane P. University of Vermont, "Amy Lowell and the Music of Her Poetry". The New England Quarterly, Vol. 6, No. 1 (March 1989), pp. 45-62. A violinist, with the source of his love for the violin in Hungary, came to New York in 1881. Charles Martin Loeffler(1861- 1935) became first violinist for the Boston Symphony. He subsequently left, to write his own music. .." Engel, Lowell and Gardner triumph over Rosenfeld in the rpesent era...for Loeffler and his frigid, philistine contemporaries are now at the center of an active and exciting renewal of interest in the Boston School of Composers, and Rosenfeld has taken a fairly obscure, if respected placed in the annals of music criticism." P. 61. See also: "A Musical Apprentice: Amy Lowell to Carl Engel. William C. Bedford. The Musical Quarterly, Vol. 58, No. 4 (Oct., 1972), pp. 519-542.
13. *Lowell, "Some Musical Analogies in Modern Poetry", The Music Quarterly, Vol. 6No. 1(Jan, 1920), pp 127-157.*
14. Ambrose, pp. 45-62.
15. Schwartz, p. 151.

16. Ibid. I own a 1st edition of *What's O'Clock* along with most of her original works, though not a copy of *Fir Flower Tablets*, and always wondered why her books were worth so little in the Antiquarian book trade. New England lyricists, Edna St. Vincent Millay, and Sara Teasdale, share a similar fate.
17. Wood, Frances. "The Lure of China. Writers from Marco Polo to J.G. Ballard". Joint Publishing Co. Ltd and Yale University Press. 2009.
18. Schwartz p.150
19. David Hinton. The Selected poems of Li Po. "Listening to a Monk's Ch'in Depths" Ch'ang-an and Middle Years. (A.D. 742-755)p 73. By permission of New Directions Books.
20. Imagism succeeded the French Symbolists, emphasizing visual evidence and images, eschewing outmoded romantic attitudes, Pound's "In a Station of the Metro" reads: *"The apparition of these faces in the crowd; petals on a wet black bough"* is a classical citation. Early Modernism defined by T.E. Hulme, and Pound himself, focussed on freedom of form, revolt from tradition, and above all the presentation of *"an intellectual and emotional complex in an instant of time"*. William Carlos Williams, a physician and poet, would say, *"no reality but in things"*, and among the Modernists, sought to paint color, images and music into his own poems. Pound will turn to the Vorticists, joining forces with Canadian-born painter Wyndham Lewis, : "The image is not an idea. It is a radiant node or cluster; it is what I can, and must perforce, call a VORTEX, from which, and through which, and into which, ideas are constantly rushing." Cubism and Futurism will emerge from the geometry of the Vorticist Art. I wrote a seminar paper for Paul Fussell, at the University of Pennsylvania, on a WWI sculptor and the Vorticist Rebel School. Most members died in the war.
21. Bynner went to China in 1917 for four months. Bynner,at age 35,took a teaching position at Berkeley, where he met a visiting Chinese scholar, Jiang Kang Hu, and with him, in a ten year long project, designed to translate the Three Hundred Tang Shi, Tang dynasty poems into English."Drinking Alone with the Moon" (1955) is a much discussed poem. When Critic Burton Watson reviewed Bynner's Jade Mountain, 1929, he felt it has a *'few serious errors, but the lapses are rare. Bynner shows*

"almost impecceable restraint" in the matter of flourishes, grace notes and embroideries on the originals,, a constant temptation for translators. Bynner also employs the use of alien place names <u>to add seasoning.</u>"The Way of Life According to Lao Tze. (James Kraft, University of New Mexico Press, 1995).

22. *Florence Ayscough & Amy Lowell: Correspondence of a Friendship by Harley Farnsworth MacNair(husband of Florence) by Jean Catel, Modern Philology Vol 44, No. 2(Nov. 1946) pp. 132-33.* Lowell writes to Asycough, August 16, 1919: "*The best translation of all is Waley's, and he hardly gives anything of Li T'ai Po's and personally, considering how greatly you improved upon all of Waley's translation, I do not think it matters if we duplicate some of the things he has used...We are to give other things from those Waley has given, and do those in which we duplicate his choice better than he has done them.*"

23. From Amy Lowell's introduction to Fir Flower Tablets, she writes, "*I have been guided somewhat by existing translations, but not wishing to duplicate what has already been adequately done, when so much still remains untouched...except for Mr. Waley's admirable work, English renderings have usually failed to convey the flavor of the originals.*"

24. Arthur Waley, admired by both Amy and Florence, Waley lived in Tokyo, Japan, and is remembered most, for his translation of the Japanese classic *The Tale of Genji*, which stood as the best translation well through the 20th century. A literary critic Raymond Mortimer would comment that Waley "felt so much at home in Tang China and Heian Japan, that he (Waley) could not face the modern ugliness amid which one has to seek out the many intact remains of beauty." Ivan Morris,Madly Singing in the Mountains. London, Allen and Unwin, 1970, p. 103.

25. Arthur Waley who graduated King's College, Cambridge, was awarded for his genius in translation, in receipt of the Queens Medal, in 1953. The British Museum published two volumes of his translations: *A Hundred and Seventy Chinese Poems* and *More Translations from the Chinese in 1919, along with Lao Tze, The Way.* Waley would revise the Chinese poems two decades later, after their publication and after the death of Amy Lowell and the publication of Fir Flower Tablets. In the 1946 edition, dedicated to Edith Sitwell, Waley, says, "*These*

revised poems work well in a literal *but at the same time* literary *translation... "My methods have changed a good deal in the last thirty years...Out of the Chinese five word line I developed between 1916 and 1923 a metre, based on what Gerald Manley Hopkins called "sprung rhythm", which I believe to be just as much an English metre as blank verse. The Chinese seven word line is more difficult to handle and I have not attempted any long poems in this metre..."* (pb edition, 1946).

26. Bonnie Kime Scott is a professor of women's studies at San Diego State University. She has written several books on gender and modernism. She reweaves Amy Lowell into Modernism's essential fabric. She closely examines the correspondence between DH Lawrence and Lowell to demonstrate *"how a cordial supportive relationship between these two volcanic personalities fit into a modernist network..."*. p. xxii Intro. Bradshaw, Melissa. Amy Lowell, American Modern, Ed. by Adrienne Munich and Melissa Bradshaw. Rutgers University Press, New Brunswick, NJ.2004

27. Ayscough writes, in From A Mirror, *"One of the means by which I have striven to attain this end is through strict observance of idiom in translation; believing, as I do, that the genius of a language appears in its idiom, I have done my utmost to preserve that of the Chinese".*

28. *"On Translating Chinese Poetry, ASIA, Dec. 1921* Bynner further contested Ayscough's transliterations and Lowell's adaptations. When Bynner had 16 poems published in the February 1925 POETRY, his accompanying article cautioned against overemphasizing the component radicals of Chinese characters when translating, by saying, *"To drag out from an ideograph its radical metaphor lands you in a limbo-language".*

29. Asycough became known for her prodigious publications on Chinese cultural customs and literature, as independent scholarship...including her celebrated biography of Tu Fu. She was the first librarian of the North branch of the Royal Asiatic Society and one of the first woman elected to its Council. On Eleanor Pearlstein and Ayscough's collection, Chicago Art Institute, see Fiona Lindsay Shen, "Florence Asycough's Grass Hut by the Yellow Reach".

30. Lowell's biographer offers an overview of the working

partnership. "An expert Sinologue, she(Asycough) also had the services of Mr. Nung Chu, who, though he knew no English, gladly furnished her with all the apparatus of the scholia as well as the analyses of the written characters, the importance of which Miss Lowell had discovered during Mrs. Ayscough's visit in June, 1918. Mrs. Ayscough would prepare a word –for-word translation of each poem, with expansion, explanations and references added in red ink, all of which was followed by an analysis of each character into its roots, various meanings and implications. From this complicated manuscript, Miss Lowell would work, writing her poem line for line with the original, then sending her version to Mrs. Ayscough. Some poems would turn out satisfactorily in half an hour; others crossed and recrossed America and the Pacific several times before they were right. When Mrs. Ayscough came to Sevenels, they would go over all the manuscripts that had been completed since they met last." (DAMON, p. 587)

31. On August 9, 1921 Florence Asycough came to town and the women put in three weeks of solid work on the Chinese poetry. An appendix of notes and an elaborate appendix of note and cross references of words had to be constructed. The Introduction was finished and sent off on the 29th. ...Jessie Rittenhouse called one afternoon, and was told to "come right out". When she arrived, she was waved to a chair, and told "We are finishing Fir Flower Tablets." She found her busy at work with Mrs. Ayscough. Bubbling with animation, Miss Lowell explains that though her physican had forbidden her to work, she was determined to get Fir Flower Tablets on the market before Witter Bynner's Jade Mountain... She then read Miss Rittenhouse some of the poems; never had she read with more creative fire – it was almost as though she herself had written these antique poems. Damon p. 573.

32. "AMY LOWELL: The World of Amy Lowell and the Imagist Movement" Richard Benvenuto. 1985." There was too much exposition and long "winded" titles and Amy felt the book was a "professional mistake". The poems lacked color and luster.

33. Remy de Bourmont, Amy Lowell, "Six French Poets: Studies in Contemporary Literature", Macmillan, 1915.

34. Most popular and reissued in five subsequent editions in France in 1902, 1908, 1928, 1933, and most recently, 2004. The Book of

Jade has since been translated into German, English, Italian, Portuguese, Spanish, Polish and Russian – and has provided the basis for another popular anthology of Chinese poetry in French... Victor Hugo thanked Gautier for the "exquisite work" she had sent him, and Voltaire thought he detected some "France in this China, and your alabaster in this porcelain" (16 June 1867) qtd in Richardson 57. At another point, Voltaire remarked in a letter to Gautier, (1869)"Going to China is like going to the moon"(Daniel 7) FN(465) Pauline Yu. "Your Alabaster in This Porcelain": Judith Gautier's Le Livre de Jade". PMLA, pp 464-482.2007 (p 471 Pauline Yu) "This incidentally prefigures a controversial method later employed by Florence Ascough and Amy Lowell in the 1921 collaboration, Fir Flower Tablets, and described in the volume's introductory essay as a "split-up" of a character to foreground its visual effect" (lxxxix-xcii).
35. *These translations are poems, they are as much Miss Lowell's as they are Li T'ai po's."* Archibald MacLeish, from "Amy Lowell and the Art of Poetry", North American Review, March, 1925, p. 520
36. Carolyn Forche, Forward. See book review by Janet Roberts. http://www.idest-journal.com Tetova University, Macedonia. 2009.

SOURCES CONSULTED:

Ambrose, Jane P. Amy Lowell and the Music of her Poetry The New England Quarterly, Vol 62 No 1(March 1989) pp. 45-62

Benevenuto, Richard. AMY LOWELL. Michigan State University, Twayne, Boston, 1985. Chapter Six. Imagists and Impressionists: The Major Lyrics. and p. 27, "The Life of Amy Lowell." And "Active Invalid", p. 312.

Bradshaw, Melissa. Selected Poems of Amy Lowell. "Amy Lowell, New American Poet". Rutgers University Press, 2005.

Bradshaw, Melissa and Munich, Adrienne. Amy Lowell, American Modern. Rutgers University Press, New Brunswick, NJ 2004

Catel, Jean. "Florence Asycough & Amy Lowell: Correspondence of a Friendship" by Harley Farnsworth MacNair. Modern Philology, Vol 44, Nov. 1946, pp. 132-22.

Cawes, Marianne. "On the Horizontal: Women Writing on Writing Women". The Changing Profession.PMLA,Modern Language

Association. pp. 549-557. 2007

Christie, Stuart. "Disorientations: Canon without Context in Auden's "Sonnets from China". PMLA. Modern Language Association, pp. 1576-1587, New York. 2005. Demands of English-ness avoids "orientalization", negotiating cultural meaning.

Damon, Foster. AMY LOWELL, . Chapter XXII "Fir Flower Tablets and a Hoax for Distraction".Boston: Houghton Mifflin Company, 1935.

Fenollosa, Ernest. The Chinese Written Character as a Medium for Poetry. 1918. San Francisco: City Lights, 1936.

Flint, F. Cudworth. Univ of Minnesota Press, Pamphlets of American Writers. No. 82. 1969. P. 32-35

Forche, Carolyn. Foreword. Xxvii-xxxiii.LANGUAGE FOR A NEW CENTURY. Contemporary Poetry from the Middle East, Asia and Beyond. W.W. Norton & Co. New York,.London. 2007

Gould, Jean. Amy The World of Amy Lowell and the Imagists Movement. Dodd & Mead, NY, 1975. The impassioned heart of Amy Lowell's poetry.

Hayot, Eric. "Critical Dreams: Orientalism, Modernism, and the Meaning of Pound's China", Twentieth Century Literature. 45.4 (1999).

Healey, Claire. "Some Imagist Essays: Amy Lowell." The New England Quarterly. Vol. 43. No. 1. March 1970. Pp. 134-138.

Hinton, David. Translator. The Selected Poems of Li Po. New York: New Directions, 1996. Winner of the 1997 Harold Morton Landon Translation Award. The Selected Poems of Wang Wei, New Directions, 2006, Funded by a Guggenheim Foundation Grant and Mountain Home. The Wilderness Poetry of Ancient China. New Directions, 2002. Reprinted here with the permission of New Directions Press.

Kennedy, George A. "Fenollosa, Pound and the Chinese Character". Yale Literary Magazine, Vol. 126, no. 5. December 1958.

Lawrence, D.H. Selected Letters. Intro. Diana Trilling. New York: Farrar, Strauss, Cudahy, 1958.

Lefevre, Andre. Constructing Cultures. Ed. Susan Bassnett & Andre Lefevere. Multi-Lingual Matters. Philadelphia. Joannesburg Sydney Tokyo Cleveden. Pp 12-25. "Chinese and Western Thinking on Translation"; Chinese centrality and of acculturating the other, on its own terms). "Transplanting the Seed", Susan Bassnett. Pp. 63-64. Pound stresses target language and " Melopoeia, phanopoeia and Iogopoeia".

Lowell, Amy. Fir Flower Tablets. Poems Translated from the Chinese by Florence Ayscough Hon. Mem. North China Branch, Royal Asiatic Society. English Versions by Amy Lowell. Boston and New York Houghton Mifflin Company, Copyright 1921, by Florence Ayscough and Amy Lowell http://digital.library.upenn.edu/women/lowell/tablets.html.

Lowell, "A Dome of Many Colored Glass": Boston: Houghton Mifflin, 1912. Pictures of the Floating World. New York: Macmillan, 1919. What's O'Clock, Boston: Houghton Mifflin, 1925. "Some Imagist Poets. Boston, Houghton Mifflin, 1915-1917. Vols.I.II. and III. "On Three Chinese Poets", Lecture. 1922.

Liu, James J. Y. The Art of Chinese Poetry. Chicago: The University of Chicago Press, 1962.

McNair, Harley Farnsworth. Florence Ayscough & Amy Lowell. : Correspondence of a friendship. "Chicago: Univ of Chicago Press, 1945.

Moore, Honor. Selected Poems. Introductory essay xv-xxxiii Library of America. 2004.

Perrine, Laurence. American Literature, Vol. 47. No. 3(Nov. 1975) pp. 471-472. .

Red Pine, Translator. POEMS OF THE MASTERS. China's Classic Anthology of T'ang and Sun Dynasty Verse. Copper Canyon Press 2003.

Rexroth, Kenneth. "The Poetry of the Far East in a General Education." Approaches to the Classics, Ed. William Theodore de Bary, Columbia University Press, 1959. Also, "WomenPoets of China" and "Women Poets of Japan".

Rollyson, Carl. "The Absence of Amy Lowell", New Criterion. Vol. 26. Issue l. September 2007.

Ruihley, Glenn Richard. The Thorn of a Rose. Amy Lowell Reconsidered. "The Discovery of Form, p. 98-105. Archon Books, Hamden, Ct. Shoe String Press. 1975. Pp. 104-5, 120-121..

Schwartz, William Leonard."A Study of Amy Lowell's Far Eastern Verse" Modern Language Notes, Vol. 43, No. 3 (March 1928) pp. 145-152.

Steiner, George. After Babel. Aspects of Language and Translation.

Oxford University Press. 1975, 1998. Chapter 2. Language and Gnosis. Language as deep structure. Chapter 3. Word Against Object. Language as cultural system

Von Flotow, Luise. Translation and Gender. Translating in the "Era of Feminism' SFLEP. Shanghai. St. Jerome, Manchester, England, and University of Ottawa Press, Canada. 1997.

Qiu Xiaolong. RED MANDARIN DRESS. NY: St Martin's Press, 2007.

Waley, Arthur. Dedicated to Edith Sitwell. Chinese Poems. Unwin Paperbacks. London, 1946.

Wood, Frances. The Lure of China. Writers from Marco Polo to J.G. Ballard. Joint Publishing Co. Ltd and Yale University Press. Chapter 15. Bloomsbury in China. Arthur Waley, p 199-202. 2009.

Young, David. Translator. Du Fu. A Life in Poetry. Alfred A. Knopf, New York 2008..

Yoshihara, Mari. Gender and Sexuality in Amy Lowell's "Asian" Poetry "Putting on th Voice of the Orient". "The Making of Amy Lowell's "Translations": Fir Flower Tablets. P 120-125. Ed. Bradshaw, Melissa and Munich, Adrienne. Amy Lowell, American Modern, Rutgers University Press, New Brunswick, NJ 2007. Mari Yoshihara, teaches womens gender studies at the University of Hawaii, Manoa. Author of "Embracing the East: White Women and American Orientalism(2002). Yoshihara maintains that Amy Lowell deliberately omitted women poets. Lowell herself said that she felt the women poets were not as good as the men poets. The character of the collaboration with Ascough is misrepresented in this article.

Yu, Pauline. "Your Alabaster in This Porcelain": Judith Gautier's Le Livre de Jade". PMLA, The Modern Language Association of America. pp 464-482.2007.

Yunte Huang, Transpacific Displacement: Ethnography, Translation and Intertextual Travel in Twentieth Century American Literature (Berkeley, CA: University of California Press, 2002). Huang cites Lowell's publications as "Ethnographical writing: intertextual travel" and "falling between scholarly ethnographic accounts and popular travel writings"... Florence Ayscough 's earned a reputation as an ethnologist, making her residency in Shanghai, cultivating her perceptions, beyond that of a tourist, by learning Chinese, and venturing successful translations. Lindsay Shen takes up this subject and shows in fact how much respect Ayscough did obtain for her efforts. ... *Asycough would assert:* " *Foreigners become confused by the suggestions and allusion, because without knowledge of their referents, much of the associative meaning and beauty are lost.*" *...the words... often bring before the mind of the Occidental reader an entirely different scene to that actually descibed by the Oriental poet. The topography, the architecture, the fauna and flora, to say nothing of the social customs, are all important.*"

Transcultural routes of transpacific migration of cultural meanings" is the path scholar Huang criticizes in resentful scrutiny of Lowell's accomplishment. The fatal error she makes, however, in her observations is to confuse Ayscough's role with that of Lowell. Huang conflates Ayscough's ethnographical interest with Lowell's transformation of the material into verse form. Huang also critiques Lowell for not being a sinologist, whereas Asycough is credited with being an amateur sinologist. Huang asserts, "*As a traveler in the world of texts, the Imagist poet Lowell projected the image of the far East in a manner characteristic of a tourist's fascination with a locale rather than an old time ethnographer's devotion to a particular geographical area...*"

THE CLARK FAMILY AND WEIHAI

Zhang Jianguo and Zhang Junyong
Translated by Ma Xianghong

After the establishment of the treaty ports in modern China, many Westerners came to Weihai; its commercial development brought about great social change. The Westerners wanted to take advantage of Weihai's free port status to develop businesses. Their commercial success hastened the transformation of Weihai from a traditional agricultural society to a modern industrial and commercial one. However, for a variety of reasons most of these Western entrepreneurs have been forgotten. One example is the Clark Family, who were the first foreign investors in modern Weihai.

Duncan Clark Senior was born in Scotland in 1856 and his father farmed a small farm in Islay, called Cladville. When his father died in 1864, the family was left impoverished. Duncan, who was only eight, had to look for work and moved to Glasgow to find employment in the shipyards. After paying for his lodgings, he sent all the cash he earned to his mother, whom he adored.

Due to the special historical situation, China became a paradise for speculators and adventurers in the late nineteenth century. Lots of businessmen became rich, successful and famous, which naturally attracted Clark, who was eager to change a difficult financial situation. He finally left the shipyard and came to China alone. However, although a Westerner who might be presumed to enjoy advantages over native Chinese at that time, his transition in China was not a smooth one. He caught cholera, and on the verge of death he crawled from the hospital mortuary onto the street. Fortunately, two women missionaries found him and cared for him until he recovered. He lived a hard and unsettled life until he joined the Chinese Imperial Customs Service. Later, he came to the Customs Service at Chefoo where his life gradually improved, owing to his Scottish predilection for hard work and thrift. In 1892, he was awarded the Victoria Medal for Gallantry by the British Government, in recognition of his efforts with five others, to prevent loss of life on board the barge "Stanfield" of London, during a fierce gale. The following April he married Annie Newman, 14 years his junior, and the daughter of the founder of a family hotel at Chefoo. This marriage was to be of great benefit to him.

In the late nineteenth century, various kinds of foreign funds came into China's market. The major powers' fights over their interests in China were intensifying. Britain leased Weihaiwei, an important port in northern China, as a naval base, in order to contend with Russia at Port Arthur. Before that, Britain's range of influence was confined to southern China and Changjiang Valley; thus it was disadvantaged in relation to the efforts of Russia, Germany and other countries to carve up northern and northeastern China. The lease of Weihaiwei in 1898 made a breach for British funds flowing northwards, and greatly stimulated its desire for expansion. Clark, attracted by such an environment, believed that Weihaiwei would be a better place to develop business. In the same year he left the Customs Service-Chefoo and moved to Weihaiwei, only 60 miles from Chefoo. With his accumulated savings he founded the first foreign firm in modern Weihai, D. Clark & Co. on Liugong Island.

In the early days of D. Clark & Co, the British government hadn't assumed full control of Weihaiwei. Clark supplied the British military and Western residents with beef, vegetables and other daily necessities. He installed a steam bakery and supplied the Navy with bread. The range of business was limited, but successful due to the stable market. His first big chance came in 1900 during the Boxer Uprising. At that time, eight major powers formed an allied force in order to suppress the Boxers. The majority of British troops were fighting in the Boer War in South Africa, and no troops could be sent to China. Thus the Chinese Regiment at Weihaiwei was sent to the Northern China fields and the Indian unit of the British expeditionary force also went northwards via Weihaiwei. These troops lacked rear services—an essential component of a modern army, so Clark chartered a ship, loaded it with provisions and traveled north with the force. Through this expedition Clark not only greatly profited, but also established good relations with the military. When he returned to Weihai, he got all the naval contracts for feeding the Navy. Each summer, the British China Fleet came to Weihaiwei for rest and exercises, and D. Clark & Co. provided almost all the rear services to the fleet. When British policy on Weihaiwei changed, Duncan took advantage of the opportunity to become the largest tourism investor at Weihai.

In terms of commercial impact, Britain's occupation attracted both positive and negative comment. However, the area was unanimously agreed to have an excellent climate and natural environment, and was regarded as 'the most suitable place to be a health resort within the United Kingdom'. Shortly after the lease of Weihaiwei, Britain spent 250 million pounds on the war in South Africa, which impeded further Government expenditure on the construction of the naval base at Weihaiwei; additionally, the international situation changed rapidly. Therefore, in 1902 Britain formally announced that it would give up plans for the construction of the Weihaiwei naval base, and that the territory would only be used as a summer station for the Navy for rest and exercises. From then on, except during the First World War, the China Fleet at Hong Kong came to Weihaiwei from the end of April to the end of October each year. Many European residents in other parts of China also spent summers at Weihaiwei, which gradually became a famous summer resort well-known by Europeans in China.

Astutely, Clark established a hotel at the suggestion of his wife. At first they rented the building formerly used as Chinese naval officers' quarters. The Island Hotel catered specifically to Westerners, including British naval officers' wives and children; the building was later reconstructed on the same site, and in the early 1930s the one-floor hotel was converted into a two-floor building. In 1906 when the Chinese Regiment was disbanded, Clark rented the

Regiment officers' quarters to start a hotel on the mainland. These two hotels won high recognition by 1908. The Island Hotel still survives in good condition. From its imposing façade, it is easy to imagine its period of prominence. However, Clark's biggest and most successful investment in tourism was the purchase of the King's Hotel at Port Edward. It was formerly named the Queen's Hotel, and had been built for Lawers & Clark Co. by the Weihaiwei Land and Building Company Ltd. The Shanghai Astor Hotel managed it in 1902 and invested 250,000 dollars on an extension and improvements. This hotel had 80 large bedrooms, private dining rooms in addition to the large public dining-hall, and all the appurtenances of a first-class hotel. There was a special bathing beach, a pier, a launch and tennis courts. Each summer, the band of the Astor House came from Shanghai to perform in the concert-hall on the ground floor.

Clark's purchase of this hotel has become part of local lore. During the lease period, Weihaiwei became a haven for various kinds of figures. Early in the lease period, Japan invaded Korea, and many Koreans came to Weihaiwei or passed through the territory to other refuges. The charismatic Clark became very friendly with a Korean General Ming, one member of Queen Mingcheng's family. General Ming persuaded Clark to attempt to rescue the Korean Emperor, who was a prisoner of the Japanese. Clark chartered a sea-going tug from Shanghai and steamed across from Weihai to the Korean coast, but failed to rescue the Emperor. When he returned to Weihai, there was a hotel for sale, the King's Hotel on the mainland. General Ming thought it would be a fitting place for the Emperor's residence, so he purchased it with Clark. Within three years Clark bought Ming out, and became sole owner. Many years later, the King's Hotel became one of the most famous coastal hotels in China, mentioned in many contemporary publications.

By the late 1920s, D. Clark & Co. had become the most powerful investor in Weihai, covering tourism, public amenities, transport, land property, farming, education, and other areas. In the areas of commerce and trade, D.

Clark & Co. dealt mainly in export, and owned many stores and warehouses on both Liugong Island and the mainland, being the biggest wholesaler of coal and foreign goods. In public amenities, it was the sole agent of the Hong Kong General Post Office at Weihai, managing two post offices on the island and the mainland that encompassed the whole postal service of the territory; in the transportation sector, it managed a barge company, supplied drinking water to ships, built two special tourist piers, was the earliest company to run a ferry service between the mainland and the island, and was an early supplier of transportation services between Weihai and Chefoo. Additionally, it planted vegetables and exotic fruits for local and distant markets.

As the founder and general manager, Duncan Clark assumed a prestigious social and administrative position in the territory. He was not only the senior member of the Advisory Council, but held important positions in several clubs and societies. At the end of the 1920s, Clark gave the Island Hotel to his eldest son Jack, and the King's Hotel to his second son, Donald, then took his wife back to Scotland, where he bought the Island of Eriska and lived there until he died in 1939.

Previously, within academic discourse in China, this type of foreign commercial activity was considered the outcome of the imperialist economic invasion of China, and believed to have succeeded through the exploitation of the working people and privileges of unfair treaties; it was seldom considered as an investment within a specific historic and business context. In fact, although Weihaiwei at that time was under direct British rule and enjoyed free port status, its investment environment didn't attract internal or foreign funds. For the British government, Weihai was only a bargaining chip in a wider political strategy; thus from the start of occupation, the lease period was not fixed. Further, Weihaiwei was administered at low cost. These problems made it difficult to improve transportation and education, invest in infrastructure and enact social progress. Particularly from 1905, the issue of the return of

Weihaiwei was often proposed, and Britain clearly refused to offer political guarantees for any investment at Weihai. Therefore, no funds came to Weihai from 1906 onwards, and some available investment was withdrawn. In general, there was not much foreign investment in Weihai—not more than seven or eight firms. Under such circumstances, the establishment and success of D. Clark & Co. cannot be separated from Clark's excellent vision and business acuity. In addition, as the largest foreign firm in Weihai, D. Clark & Co. set an example in the management of funds, technology and administration. Lots of Chinese merchants learned from Clark directly or indirectly, and gradually made their own success. Thus from the perspective of the industrial and commercial development of Weihai, D. Clark and Co. was a catalyst—a fact that has caused some discomfort to some Chinese commentators.

Similarly, foreign merchants were previously considered pawns in the imperialist invasion of China, and rarely considered outside of their role as businessmen. Their character, cultural involvement, social interactions and thoughts on China were ignored. Duncan Clark's business career started and developed in Weihai. He lived there for more than twenty years and seven of his nine children and grandchildren were born there. The Clark family member who lived the longest time in Weihai stayed there for more than forty years. This family cherished a special connection to Weihai over their long residence here. Besides enjoying commercial success, Duncan Clark was also well known for his charitable work which included starting a free island school for Chinese children. At that time, because of lack of funds and suspicion of radical trends, the colonial authorities did not encourage modern—especially British—education for Chinese children. Duncan Clark, however, embraced the concept. Early in 1904 he founded the King's School on Liugong Island, free for Chinese children, offering English, Business and other modern courses. More than 50 children attended the school for the first school year, which almost topped all Weihai schools in the attendance scale. Duncan's second son, Donald, managed the King's Hotel.

His feelings towards Weihai exceeded those of his father. His family members regarded him more a Chinese than a Scot. He loved China more deeply than Britain.

Donald Clark was born in Weihai in 1901 and was educated in Weihaiwei School. He began to manage the King's Hotel in the 1930s, and returned home in 1939 to fight in World War 11. On the outbreak of the Pacific War, he asked to go to the Asian battle field to fight against Japan. He returned to live in Britain after the war and died in 1975 in Scotland. About 40 years in Weihai sowed the seed of love towards this place in Donald's heart. He had great sympathy for the Chinese people during those hard days. Reviewing the records about Donald, what moved the author deeply is that he tried hard to help Weihai people fight against the Japanese early in the conflict.

Japan invaded Weihai in 1938. Sun Xifeng, High Commissioner of the Weihaiwei Municipal Government, left Weihai without permission. The acting High Commissioner and Chief Constable Zheng Weiping led a force to withdraw to the countryside and insisted on fighting against the Japanese army. At that time, Donald Clark was in a pivotal position because of his British background and his family's influence in Weihai. Various parties wanted to draw him into the situation. He was well-connected, and was especially close to Zheng Weiping. Zheng was from Hebei Province and had graduated from the Beijing Model Army Regiment. He acted as Weihai's Chief Constable in 1936 and attended the Lushan Officer Training Class, organized by Jiang Jieshi. After Japanese troops came to Weihai in 1938, he led the force to fire the first shot at the Japanese. By 1939, he was appointed Commissioner of the 7th Administrative Zone of Shandong Province and Commander responsible for public security. He incorporated more than 10,000 men into his own force and led the fight against the Japanese army; thus his troops became the main anti-Japanese force of Weihai. Later, when the war had reached a stalemate, Zheng's force fought Mao's troops as well as the Japanese. They attacked the Eighth Route Army and killed the Communist leaders. In 1942, Zheng's force was pursued by Japanese troops because of Zheng's attack on the Japanese on Liugong Island. Then they ambushed the Eighth Route Army at Cuixiakou Valley in Wendeng. Finally, Zheng escaped to Chongqing to act as a counselor of the Nationalist Government. Later he became a member of the Hebei Provincial Committee and also held other positions such as liaison officer at Peking. He was arrested in 1949 and executed at Wendeng in 1954.

Zheng Weiping has been a figure banished to the peripheries of history. But for the Scot Donald Clark, Zheng was a gentleman of honesty, firmness and national integrity. Donald Clark not only sent Zheng's wife and son to Tianjing to take refuge there in the British Consulate just before the Japanese invaded Weihai, but also secretly offered him information, ammunition, medicine and provisions during his war with Japan. When the British Consul at Weihaiwei requested him to stop assisting Zheng, and to persuade Zheng not to raid Weihai again, Donald refused flatly with the excuse, "the man is fighting for his existence." Zheng's frequent raids on Weihai were very troublesome to the Japanese, so Zheng was offered quarter of a million dollars and 500 troops if he surrendered, and Donald ten percent of this sum if he could help persuade Zheng. Donald refused immediately: "not all Chinese will do anything for dollars. Zheng is straight as a die, I can't persuade a man to go against his conscience. I will most likely insult him when I make the suggestion." Under Japanese pressure, Donald slipped into Zheng's area as a gesture. Zheng's reply to him was, "I am a Chinese, I love my nation and hate Japanese. Since the war broke out, I will continue to fight firmly." Donald made many further efforts to help Zheng. He was often outspoken about his enemies, and was at one time mistaken for a criminal and almost murdered on the streets of Weihaiwei.

Duncan Clark's eldest son, John, was the last family member who left Weihai. John was born in Chefoo in 1897 and began to manage the Island Hotel and other business of D. Clark & Co. in the late 1930s. A few elderly Weihai residents still retain memories of John. He suffered from a stroke which made him lame at 39, thus the local people called him 'Lame Zhang' (the same pronunciation as 'Lame John'.) His Island Hotel was also called 'The Lame Hotel' or 'Lao Zhang Hotel'. John ardently loved hunting. He often hunted foxes in the mountains of Weihaiwei. According to a local saying, it was a fox spirit that made him lame. Perhaps because he stayed in Weihai for such a long period, he believed in the local customs, so he had a fox tattooed on his back to pray for an early recovery. After the death of his father, John as the eldest son followed the Scottish custom, and returned to Scotland to inherit his father's property in 1940. John Clark died in Nottingham in 1948.

Since John returned to Scotland in 1940, the Clark Family has been away from Weihai for more than 60 years. The Clark descendents can appreciate the legacy of their family through memory and surviving imposing buildings. Duncan Clark, Junior, the eldest son of Donald Clark, reintroduced the family to Weihai after the absence of so many years.

Duncan was born in Weihai in 1935 and left Weihai with his father in 1938. He is retired and lives now in Coventry, England. We first met Duncan at his home during the Spring Festival of 2002, when we were collecting historical records in England. He warmly showed us several hundred old photographs of his family and China taken from the late nineteenth century until the 1940s, along with other collections. He shared with us many memories of his grandparents and parents. His love and affection for Weihai showed clearly in his words and manner.

Duncan left Weihai when he was only four years old, so almost all his memories came from his parents' stories and family collections of old photographs and documents. He said that Weihaiwei and China had been the topic of family conversation, especially during his father's final illness, which touched him greatly. Donald Clark suffered a stroke in 1967, and was absorbed in memories of Weihai for the rest of his life. His son was moved by his father's deep love of Weihai, and felt sad that he failed to meet his wish to return.

From then on, Duncan devoted time and effort to his family's history. During his father's illness, he recorded his father's reminiscences about Weihai and China. Through our contact with Duncan, we feel his honesty, kindness and affection toward Weihai. Since our first meeting, he has collected archival material for us, and personally paid all the relevant costs. He has given our Archives several hundred old photographs and nearly a hundred historical documents. One of the things that moves us deeply is that he donated the territory flag of Weihaiwei to our Archives.

Before we met Duncan, we had learnt from a Taiwanese friend that there had existed a territory flag of Weihaiwei under British rule, but we had never had the opportunity to see an original. However, at Duncan's home in 2002, he showed us the flag kept by the Clark family. We showed very great interest in it on the spot. Later we wrote to him and asked him to reproduce one for us in England. In May 2004, we visited Duncan again during a Weihai government trip to Europe. Unexpectedly, he gifted us the original flag, which had been treasured by the family for almost one century. What a very big excitement! What a selfless Gentleman! He just kept the replica instead. Later, he told us that he decided during our first meeting to present the flag to us some day, because he thought that Weihai was the proper place to keep it, where it could be appreciated and get the best care. During these recent years, we have been working for the collection and preservation of Weihai historical archives that are now scattered abroad. We have travelled and experienced a lot, including four trips to England, but seldom received anything original as a gift. Sometimes, we considered ourselves lucky if the current owners revealed what material they had.

In consideration of Duncan Clark's great effort for us, we intended to include a special thanks to him in the epilogue of our book *Weihaiwei under British Rule*, but he said, "I'm just a tie between you and my forefathers, anything that I did is what I should do. No honour is needed." When we expressed in our invitation letter that we would offer him free accommodation during his stay in Weihai, he refused firmly and expressed clearly, "I would hate you to think that anything I had given you, had been given with the expectation that I would get something in return. I can assure you that thought has never entered my mind. I do not want to take advantage of your hospitality; otherwise, I would just stay for a very short period."

Duncan also had some hesitation in offering us some information. For example, when we listened to Donald Clark's recordings on two tapes at Duncan's home in 2002, we asked him to reproduce one set for us and he readily agreed. But it was difficult to understand Donald's pronunciation due to his old age and Scottish accent, so we wrote to request a transcript. Unexpectedly, he spoke frankly in the answering letter that the posted tapes had some omissions because he was afraid that some of his father's views would not be accepted by the contemporary Chinese. We realized immediately that the value of the original information probably exceeded these misgivings, thus we insisted on getting the originals. Finally, he mailed us the new tapes and transcriptions, and explained, "some of the views expressed by my father may not be too popular in modern China but these were his honestly held views, based on his own experiences at that time." After reading the transcription, we realized that these unpopular views were expressed in the section about the anti-Japanese fight at Weihai, and we realized that much confusion and misunderstanding existed over each parties' viewpoints.

From September 28 to October 13, 2004, Duncan came to Weihai together with his wife and youngest son, who was in Australia on business. During their stay, we accompanied them to the historical sites and to visit old friends. He said that every day here was full of excitement, unexpected things and pleasant surprises. It's true that he was moved by daily experiences and we were moved by his feelings. One day, we took him to see some old houses in the poorer district on the historic Qixia Street, so that he could see traces of the old Weihaiwei. We knocked at a door at random, and an old lady in rags came out. Unexpectedly she was Li Yuying, a daughter of Li Yizhi, who had been a good friend of Donald Clark. Li Yizhi was from Zhongshan, Guangdong Province and came to Weihaiwei during the British lease period. He was the comprador of D. Clark & Co. and owned the Tailai Firm at that time. He became the Chairman of the Commercial Chamber at Port Edward in the late 1920s and was one of a few famous figures in Weihai. After the victory against the Japanese in 1945, he was employed as an interpreter by the Eighth Route Army in Weihai, and attended the negotiation to prevent the landing of the American Pacific Fleet. Later he became a member of the Administrative Council of Weihaiwei, and then went to Hong Kong. Most of his children finished higher education. For example, Li Yuying graduated from Furen University in Peking in the 1940s.

Li Yizhi had a close relationship with the Clark Family. On his return home, Donald Clark made a special request to his younger brother, who acted as Australian Minister in China, to search for Li Yizhi. He still talked about Li just before his death. Before Duncan's trip, we had planned to contact Ms. Li for a meeting with him, but it was difficult to reach her, as she had no permanent home. That day their meeting seemed destined. And, surprisingly, Li Yuying could talk with Duncan in fluent English. Seeing Li Yuying in rags and her poor rented house, Duncan couldn't keep back his tears. The crowd of onlookers was also touched by the scene and their affection. In the large yard of the Island Hotel, the familiar sight struck a chord in his heart. Duncan sat there quietly for a long moment, staring at the old building without a word. Then he paced up and down slowly. Watching his excitement and figure, the author suddenly felt that this was not a return trip of one generation, but of three generations, across a century.

This article is mainly based on the private archives of the Clark Family, including Donald Clark's final recording. Though Donald's thoughts bear his personal deep feelings, they still have their unique historical and cultural value. The article is just a record in order to show respect for folk memory and affection for place.

JAPANESE PEOPLE IN MODERN SHANGHAI

CHEN ZU'EN
TRANSLATED BY CATHERINE DONGYUAN YIN

In 1943 Shanghai became a trading port due to the pressure of western powers, and gradually came to act as the source of transmitting western science eastward. The Japanese regarded Shanghai as Asia's Europe. Since the Meiji Restoration in 1868, a continuous flow of Japanese emigrants moved into Shanghai in search of opportunities. They initially sought shelter in the Western concessions but later moved to the newly-developed Hongkou area. There they established the "Japanese streets." Since the Japanese were "latecomers" to concession-era Shanghai, they were initially placed under the jurisdiction of the concessional authorities. However, the Japanese endeavoured to compete with their Western counterparts in such aspects as political, economical and cultural influences, and to build their very own "Japanese concessions."

IMMIGRANTS TO SHANGHAI FROM A WEAKER NATION
IN THE EARLY YEARS

As part of the Meiji Restoration, the prerogative of trade was abolished. The general public could freely engage in trade as well as any other vocations. The Samaria class was permitted to engage in agrarian, business, and manufacturing vocations. Western ships could be privately owned. These measures encouraged the Japanese to expand overseas. In September 1871, China and Japan entered into the *Sino-Japanese Provisions of Cordial Relations* and *Sino-Japanese Commerce Treaty*. The former was the first pact to be made by the two sides as equals. Thus the Meiji Restoration and the conclusion of the treaties fuelled Japanese emigration to Shanghai.

In 1870, seven male Japanese officially registered with the Shanghai Municipal Council. They were the first recognized Japanese expatriates. Four of them resided in the former British Concession and three in the former Hongkou American Concession. The years between 1870 and 1880 saw the slow rise in the population increase of Japanese emigrants, accounting for five or six annually, among which one third was male and the other two thirds female. Up until 1890, among the foreign population of 4,200 in Shanghai, there were only 644 Japanese (339 being male and 305 female). The majority of Western expatriates were single British males in the prime of their lives who were representatives of trade companies, rather than individuals starting their own businesses.

Western culture was embodied in city life; manners and appropriate behaviour were required to follow the social norms. Dubbed the "raw food eating lower class," the early Japanese settlers mostly came from poor economic and educational backgrounds. Their behaviour was considered ill-mannered and vulgar.

Most women either engaged in prostitution or became the concubines of Chinese or Westerners. Images of Japanese walking the streets in bath robes and clogs, and of Japanese women exposing their thighs while disembarking from ships in the ports, aroused the curiosity of the Shanghainese citizens, and created negative perceptions of improper Japanese outfits among Western citizens in Shanghai. This not only embarrassed the Western-oriented Japanese, but also ruined the reputation of the Cultural Modernization movement underway in Japan. Thus, the Japanese Consulate in Shanghai started the movement to put an end to "promiscuous, lazy and vulgar behaviour." While the Japanese gradually improved their manners and behaviour, the movements also laid the groundwork for the future assertiveness of the Japanese community in Shanghai.

FORMATION OF A JAPANESE SOCIETY AND ITS CHARACTERISTICS
The establishment of the Japanese Expatriate Organization in 1907 signalled the formation of the Japanese community in Shanghai as a highly cohesive and unified ethnic group. Initially, the Japanese opened stores among the Chinese

stores on Broadway Street (Da Ming Road), Tian Tong Road, Nan Xun Road, Wen Road (Tang Gu Road) and Zha Pu Road, concentrating in central Hongkou, springing from the Japanese Consulate and Higashi Hongan-ji ('The Eastern Temple of the Original Vow'). After the First World War, the stores expanded towards Wu Song Road, Han Bi Li Road (Han Yang Road), Min Hang Road, Miller Road (E. Mei Road) and Kun Shan Road, and the area was later dubbed the "Japanese Streets."

In the column *International Image Within the Concessions in Shanghai*, it was pointed out that China's Shanghai was in Nan Shi and Zha Bei Districts, but the foreign Shanghai was in Xia Fei Road, Yang Shu Pu, Nanjing Road and Hongkou. Among the 15 photos chosen to represent "foreign Shanghai", the one for the Japanese streets featured a Japanese woman walking down Wu Song Road. The column read "arriving at Wu Song Road, one will get the impression that one has arrived in Japan rather than Shanghai, with women in kimonos, Japanese flags, shop signs of叮井 and Murakami, red sakuras and getas."

Wu Song Road was the centre of "Japanese streets" in Hongkou. On both sides of the streets, were such stores as 至诚堂book store, 长岛洋行, while inside the alleys were the Japanese residential neighbourhoods. The new Japanese streets had come into being in the 1920s, with the increase in numbers of large Japanese corporations, many corporation residences were built on North Si Chuan Road, north of Yokohama Bridge and 千爱里. According to the customary language of the Japanese expatriates, Hongkou referred to Wu Song Road and North Hongkou to North Si Chuan Road. A few Japanese also lived in East of Shanghai (Yang Shu Pu) and West of Shanghai (Xiao Sha Du), the outskirts of the Japanese textile plant area.

After many years of settlement, the Japanese in Shanghai had built a unique and full community in terms of administration management, education, religion, social welfare, public health, entertainment and cultural diffusion, etc. It was an inclusive and self-contained community in which interaction with the outside world was not necessary, and since Japanese was the only language used, life inside the community was quite similar to that back in Japan. It was therefore more appropriate to define the Japanese community as "a state within a state," rather than the Western concessions.

The highest authority in the Shanghai Japanese community was the Japanese Consulate. The Consular-general had the authority to issue decrees and the Consulate had its own police force, hence consular jurisdiction could be exercised if any Japanese were involved in civil or criminal legal conflicts with local Chinese. It was also the responsibility of the police to ensure that the expatriates followed Consulate decrees. The expatriate group was an autonomous group supervised by the Japanese Consulate-General in Shanghai. It was financially dependent on the large Japanese corporations in Shanghai, therefore the committee members were figures from higher social classes such as company board presidents and branch bank directors.

The education system was not only complete (including kindergarten, elementary schools, secondary schools, and vocational schools,) but also progressive for the time, with each grade in elementary school comprising about 40 pupils. The ratio of students to teachers was 30:1. The first school was the "亲爱舍" in the Higashi Hongan-ji which later changed its name into "开导学校" in 1888. In 1907, the newly established expatriate group took over and changed it into the Japanese Normal Advanced Elementary School, aka. Northern Elementary School. The school building was designed by a Norwegian architect and built in 1917. Many Japanese tourists were amazed by the western style concrete and the pupils who "went to school in rickshaws and automobiles."

Religious activities were what held together the emotional worlds of the Japanese. The co-existence of Buddhism, Shinto, and Christianity in the Shanghai Japanese community reflected the phenomenon in Japan itself. Buddhism was practiced in daily life, while the shrines were the places that the Japanese would visit in the first month of the lunar year. Alternatively, wedding ceremonies were usually Shinto or Christian. The first Japanese Shinto shrine in Shanghai was the Suwa Shrine in "六三花园," later renamed "Shanghai Shrine." Memorial services and funerals were mainly held in the Buddhism temples, such as Higashi Hongan-ji and Nishi Hongan-ji.

The Japanese Club was founded in 1904, and could provide for 500 people at the same time, with such facilities as a dining hall, common rooms, conference rooms, theatres and hotel rooms. Its building featured western architectural styles on the outside but Japanese style for the interior, symbolizing the Japanese community's integration into Shanghai, the emerging Global city. Yet the inclusive nature of the Japanese community within the international society in Shanghai drew a stark contrast to the friendly and intimate relations enjoyed within the Japanese community.

The Japanese theatres, cinemas, bars and dance halls located in Zha Pu Road and Hai Ning Road served to entertain the Japanese expatriates but they were not open to the Chinese general public. A few sushi bars also provided Geisha services to amuse their guests. The Triangle-area Open Market was a well-known market for its supply of Japanese cuisine ingredients, and was acclaimed as the biggest grocery market in Asia. Over 100 stores provided not only Japanese food but also fresh fish and vegetables imported from Nagasaki on a daily basis. The Market was surrounded by kimono shops, *geta* shops and bakeries that fulfilled the needs of the expatriates. A Nagasakian who used to live in Shanghai recalled, "With a plentiful collection of domestic Japanese goods, the Japanese residents in Shanghai had the impression that they were actually living in Japan."

The first Japanese hospital in Shanghai appeared in 1900, after the first Sino-Japanese War. The first Japanese general hospital was the 篠崎Hospital in Hongkou. Up until the 1930s, there were nearly 50 Japanese hospitals, including dentists, veterinaries and other health-care businesses. The福民医院, established in 1924, was the largest general hospital in the Japanese community, with an eight-storey concrete building, one underground and seven above. The hospital departments included Surgery, Medicine, Urology, Paediatrics, Gynaecology, Dentistry, Ophthalmology, Otolaryngology, Radiology, etc.

东和洋行, located in the serene North Su Zhou Road, was the earliest Japanese hostel. It had gained prominence when it had refused to accommodate Japanese prostitutes. It also boosted its reputation when the pro-Japanese Korean politician Kim U-June was murdered there in 1894. Some other hotels that featured western designs were also popular among the Japanese higher officials and elite who visited Shanghai. Conversely, Wu Jin Road was dubbed the Japanese hotel street because the main guests were the Japanese general public. A survey in 1926 showed that there were 29 Japanese hotels in Shanghai at that time. The many hotels provided a shield for those newly-arrived from Japan as they ambitiously planned on embarking upon their careers in Shanghai.

The many Japanese book stores and newspaper

The first Japanese shrine in Shanghai, 1912

The Japanese Club at Hongkou

agencies in Shanghai included such famous ones as the Uchiyama Bookstore and Japanese Hall bookstore, Tokyo Hall bookstore, Hara bookstore and 至诚堂 bookstore, while newspaper agencies published *Shanghai Daily News* and *Shanghai Nichi News*, etc.

To summarize, the Japanese had already established a closed community with a unique ethnic atmosphere, independent in terms of mentality and material life, and capable of surviving without interacting with the rest of the society. Thus, the type of western civilization offered by the Shanghai concessions that the Japanese were so fond of in the Meiji era hence became less desirable. Those latecomers had experienced solidarity and survived in a complicated environment, but still hoped that Shanghai would not always be a western-influenced city. They had a strong desire to transform Shanghai using the post-Meiji cultural framework.

THE COMPANY CLIQUE AND THE NATIVE CLIQUE
Within the social order of the Shanghai Japanese community, the "Company Clique" and the "Native Clique" were not congenial. Although there were no stark differences between the two sides, the Company Clique refers primarily to upper-class Japanese who were living in high-end residences in the British or French Concessions, and who usually worked as heads of large corporations, directors of bank branches,

senior officials, entrepreneurs or large company clerks. The Native Clique were lower-class Japanese living in Hongkou, Zhabei, Yang Shu Pu, and working in or owning small scale enterprises, stores, restaurants, etc.

The differences between the two sides resulted from the enduring impact of social and occupational distinctions. However, the defining difference between the two was that the Company Clique members were sojourners, and the Natives were settlers. The former's tenures determined their stay in Shanghai while the latter saw Shanghai as the place to realise their hopes of achieving higher incomes and occupational levels, and ultimately, their life goals.

The arrival and formation of the Company Clique was closely related to the success of Japanese industries in Shanghai. Mitsui Commercial Group, the largest Japanese financial plutocrat/ magnate, entered Shanghai in 1877 and started an import and export business in coal and cotton etc. After the Russo-Japanese War, Japanese large corporations entered Shanghai at an increasing rate, with Mitsubishi, Itochu, Furukawa and Takada all founding their branches in Shanghai. Nevertheless, the Japanese banking industry and textile industry did not enter Shanghai until after the First World War. Private banks included Sumitomo, Mitsui, Mitsubishi, Shanghai, 大东; specialized banks included the Specie Bank of Yokohama, Bank of Taiwan, etc. Large Japanese companies and bank branches were usually located on the Bund, in the British Concession. The inflow of large amounts of capital ensured that Shanghai became the centre of the Japanese textile industry in China. Thirty-three spinning manufactories in the 1920s expanded to include 60 factories whose equities exceeded 500,000 Japanese Yen in 1930.

The Company Clique lived in expensive and luxurious apartments and villas in the British and French concessions. They were very well-off and had Japanese house-maids (according to a survey in 1928, there were 542 Japanese house-maids in Shanghai at that time.) The director of Specie Bank of Yokohama lived in a villa "with grass tennis courts." The head of Mitsubishi Commercial Shanghai had owned a house with a swimming pool and tennis courts and a large garden. Although the Company Clique enjoyed elite status in Shanghai, they did not regard the place as their ultimate home but as a transitional step. Their jobs required them to be mobile and ready to move on. Thus, they were passers-through in Shanghai and would not put down their roots in the City.

The Native Clique comprised owners of small businesses and firms, restaurants, groceries and even those unemployed. Their objective was to relieve themselves of poverty and establish a brilliant career by mining opportunities in Shanghai. Therefore Shanghai was a second home to them. They started off their journeys as singles but formed families and had children and established their own businesses when they had settled down in Shanghai. Drawing a sharp contrast with the Native Clique, the individuals of the Company Clique did not create a family life in Shanghai.

Chinese citizens also lived on the Japanese streets where the Native Clique resided, whereas some from the Native Clique even lived in Chinese neighbourhoods. The cultural pluralism in Shanghai suited the needs of the Native Clique.

The self-employed Native Clique owned many stores, including groceries, egg shops, paper shops, stationary shops, pottery and lacquer shops, small restaurants, tailors, laundries, soya sauce shops, fish shops, watchmakers, bakeries, photo studios, barbers, jewellery shops, hostels, umbrella shops, carpentries, auction rooms, printing mills, etc. The Native Clique not only occupied low wage jobs, but also remitted as much of their earnings as possible to their families. The reason was that over half of the Native Clique population were dependent upon their family members.

These occupations exhibited the traits of Japanese small businesses. First, the capital accumulation pattern was through hard-work and diligence, showing a sharp difference from the usual western patterns of investment; the economic power/influence they possessed should not be overlooked, due to the long-term accumulation of capital and the large supply of labour. Second, most products and services that the small businesses provided targeted the Shanghai market and the surrounding regions, principally the Japanese living in Shanghai.

The anti-Japanese sentiments of the Chinese people, caused by the Japanese invasion of China, gradually gained momentum as the Chinese waged the widespread nationalist movements. The Japanese therefore suffered an economic crisis, especially those settlers making a living in Shanghai. The Native Clique later became collaborators with the Japanese army, as they vented their discontents and hostilities towards the patriotic movements of the Chinese people; this was also one of the realities behind the lives of the Native Clique in Shanghai.

List of Works Cited

Japanese Expatriate group in Shanghai, ed. *35th Anniversary Commemorative Journal of Japanese Expatriate Group in Shanghai*, 1942.

高西贤正. *History of the Sixty years of Higashi Hongan-ji in Shanghai*, 1937.

Okita, Ichi. *History in Shanghai*, 大陆新报社, 1942.

Okita, Ichi. *Japan and Shanghai*, 大陆新报社, 1943.

Yonezawa, Hideo. *Shanghai History*, Tokyo Unebi Press, 1942.

Ikeda, Nobuo. *A hundred Stories of Shanghai*, Japanese Hall of Shanghai, updated edition, 1923.

Kim, 一勉 . *Prostitutes, Snow, Comfort Women*, 雄山关 Press Ltd., 1997.

Gangnam, 健儿 . *New Shanghai*, Japanese Press in Shanghai, 1923.

长崎日中人民两国朋友会, 上海在留邦人が造つた日本人街, 1994.

Domestic and Foreign Cotton ed. *Fifty years History of the Domestic and Foreign Cotton Ltd. Co.* ,1937.

Japanese Mail Boat ed., *Fifty years History of the Japanese Mail Boat Company*, 1935.

Name Records of Kuniaki Residents in China, Shanghai Jinfeng Agency, 1932, 1936, 1942.

Administration Bureau of Ministry of Finance, 日本人の海外活动に关する历史的调查，通卷第27册中南支篇第一分册, 1947.

Higuchi, Hirotomo. *Japanese Investment in China*, the Commercial

Press, 1959.

History of Japanese Unions in Shanghai, 1936.

Shanghai Research Society of Historical Geography, *Shanghai Research*, 1st Series, 1942.

Hirobumi, Takatsuna. *War time Shanghai, 1937-1945*, 研文出版社, 2005.

Huang, Shiquan. *Dreams about Song Nan*, from *Miscellanies of the Shanghai Trip-Dreams about Song Nan, Dreams about the Shanghai Trip*, Shanghai Ancient Books Press, 1993.

Humanities Institute of Japan Chuo University. *Sino-Japanese War*, Publishing Division of Chuo University, 1993.

BRITISH CLUBS AND ASSOCIATIONS IN OLD SHANGHAI

NENAD DJORDJEVIC

The rich expatriate social life in old Shanghai started with the British. When Britons came to Shanghai as the first foreigners, they already had some 150 years of experience in their homeland concerning how to create and operate different social clubs and institutions. All other foreigners were largely influenced by British social activities and models.

Among foreigners, the British were the first to gain extraterritorial rights, the first to establish a foreign settlement in Shanghai, the first to open a consulate, the first to open trade representative offices, and finally the first to open social clubs, sports clubs and associations. Even though the number of British citizens did not exceed 2000 in 1865, by that time they had the major economic and administrative power in the city. All other Western powers had looked at the British experience, before undertaking negotiations with the Chinese regarding their own extraterritorial rights, opening consulates and establishing commercial firms.

Britons were famed for bringing their habits to other parts in the world; almost every major British colonial city in the world had its own missionary society, racetrack, sports club and other different types of social institutions. Shanghai was not an exception in this regard. British consular officials and the members of the *London Missionary Society* were the first Britons, and the first foreigners who came to live in Shanghai. British missionaries held the first public worship service at the British Consulate in 1843; and in 1847 they opened Trinity Church as the first British Episcopal Church in Shanghai. By 1850, members of the *London Missionary Society* established "a village of their own about one mile back from the English town and each of them had a nice garden in front and were full of interesting Chinese trees."[1] The British missionaries were almost immediately engaged in charity work, opening the first hospital for Chinese in 1846. In 1850, the hospital successfully treated 9000 patients. During the next few years, missionaries from some other British societies *(English Church Mission, Chinese Religious Tract Society, British and Foreign Bible Society)* also established their branches in Shanghai. Missionaries from other countries followed the British example.

Britons also established the first sport clubs in Shanghai. As cricket was traditionally a very popular sport in England, British officials and soldiers spread it all over the world. A journalist from the *North China Herald* noticed in 1878: "as soon as the British soldier had accomplished the occupation of Cyprus…he played cricket, he established cricket clubs also in Lagos, Algeria, Egypt, India, Japan, Arabia, Zanzibar, Gibraltar, Malta, Jamaica, Barbados, Fiji and also in Shanghai in April 1858."[2] During the nineteenth century, the *Shanghai Cricket Club* owned a Victorian-style building with an exceptional stand in front of the playing field, a pavilion and a popular bar. It played matches against teams from Hong Kong, and other treaty ports in China and Japan. The *Shanghai Cricket Club* had an English and a Scottish team. These two teams played traditional annual games throughout the nineteenth century. However, other foreigners in Shanghai were not willing to play cricket.[3]

The *Shanghai Paper Hunt Club* was another mostly British sporting club in Shanghai. The British traditionally liked hunting, but since they lacked relevant animals to hunt in Shanghai, at first, they attempted to hunt one club member with a red cowl on his head. This turned out to be a failure, which lead to the creation of the paper hunt chase. The first recorded paper hunt was won by Augustus Brown on a pony called Mud. There was also an "on-foot" version of the paper hunt, but this was disbanded in 1868.[4]

British football came to be widely accepted by all foreigners in Shanghai. The first two football clubs in Shanghai were predominantly British: the *Shanghai Athletic Club* and the *Engineers*. They played the first documented match in 1879 and continued playing traditional annual games to the end of the nineteenth century. In the late nineteenth century, the best players of the *Shanghai Athletic Club,* which later took the name *Shanghai Football Club* were: Abbot, Harris, Marshall, Robertson, and Ernest Skottowe. In honor of Ernest Skottowe, the Skottowe Cup was played from 1902 until 1949 as an international competition. The most successful were the English teams, as the 16-time winners of the Skottowe cup, followed by the Scottish teams, which were the 6- time winners. In 47 years of the Skottowe cup, many other nations took part in the competition, but only the Portuguese could to some extent challenge the champions from Britain[5].

Since the eighteenth century, almost every major colonial British city had its own racetrack. Not wishing to be an exception in this regard, Britons from Shanghai organized the first race meetings in April 1848. Horseracing was accepted by both foreigners and Chinese, and there was a popular saying that "racing was a pride of Shanghai".[6] Everybody could watch horse races, but not everybody could become a member of the *Shanghai Race Club*, which was established in 1848 as a support facility at the race track. It became one of Shanghai's most prominent clubs, eventually considered as exclusive as the *Shanghai Club*. Its chairmen and functionaries were usually elected from the most prominent members of British society. On many occasions, it organized charity receptions, concerts, masquerades, children's parties and other social gatherings. It held one of the first balls in Shanghai in 1854. Since there were just a few western women in Shanghai at that time, women gave a half, a third and sometimes a quarter of a waltz to each partner.

Rowing was the first outdoor sport in Shanghai. The *Shanghai Rowing Club* was founded in 1860, and its history can be followed up to 1949. For a long time, British and Germans competed for influence over the club. The German influence decreased with the outbreak of the First World War and vanished in 1917-18. As it was once reported in the *North China Herald*, the club "continued to flourish in spite of absence of Huns".[7]

British influence was visible in many other fields. The first British amateur theater groups (*Rangers* and *Footpads*) appeared in the early 1850s.[8] They merged in 1866, when they created the *Amateur Dramatic Corps (ADC)*. The British were also the first to organize scholarly associations in Shanghai. The *Royal Asiatic Society,* with its headquarters in London, was the most important scholarly society in Shanghai. Among the first RAS members were missionaries from the *London Missionary Society,* William Lockhart, W. H. Medhurst and Alexander Wylie. Two British members of the RAS, Sir Robert Hart and Sir Harry Parkes, received the rare honor of having their statues erected in Shanghai.

Some of the most prestigious British establishments came into existence in the 1860s and 1870s. The most famous of them – the *Shanghai Club* – was soon regarded as the most exclusive establishment for Shanghai's British elite. The club reportedly had the longest bar in the world, or at least in Asia. The end near the window, looking out over the Bund, was reserved for the river pilots. Next to them, at the head of the bar, stood the wealthiest and most powerful members of British society, such as the Keswick brothers and directors of banks. The *Shanghai Library* complained that the reason for its continuous financial difficulties and lack of members was because the *Shanghai Club* had established a remarkable library, which attracted many readers. The 1932 catalogue of the non-fiction section of the *Shanghai Club's* library contained several thousand books on science, philosophy, poetry, art, history, sport, natural history, travel, China and the Far East.[9] This all–male club applied rigorous rules for membership. New applicants were carefully screened by existing members. Failure to settle monthly accounts in time resulted in immediate expulsion. The *Shanghai Club* was also a venue for many other British associations. Members of the *Shanghai Paper Hunt Club,* the *St. George Society,* the *Allied Federation of Shanghai,* the *Shanghai Clay – Pigeon Club,* the *Old Carthusian Society* and many other – mostly British – associations, held annual meetings and organized receptions at the *Shanghai Club.*

The *Country Club* was also known as an exclusive British club. It had extensive lawns, flowerbeds, fountains, a swimming pool, six billiard tables, a card room, a small theatre, ballroom, and tennis courts. It also had a successful bowling team – the *Country Club Giant Killers* that played in the Shanghai Lawn

Bowls League. A visitor, proposed and seconded by at least two members, could be admitted for a period not exceeding ten days. Some other foreigners and Chinese established their own country clubs modeled entirely on the *Country Club*. Country clubs were expected to provide "facilities that offer a variety of recreational sports opportunities to its members, mostly tennis and golf and to provide dining facilities to their members and guests." In addition to the fees, most of them had additional requirements to join and refused to admit as members those who were Chinese, Jewish or Russian. Chinese country clubs were flexible and accepted all nationalities. All of the country clubs were located in what was then the suburban area of Shanghai.[10]

Many clubs were not famed for their exclusiveness or exceptional service. The unique *Sailor's Home*, though, had dining, smoking, sleeping, reading and washing rooms. At the opening ceremony in 1860, a dinner was served to 200 British and French soldiers and sailors. Later, the guests "formed themselves into dancing parties", while a band played polkas, quadrilles and horn-pipes.[11] A similar club was the British-dominated *Captain's Club*. It was opened in the 1870s for the use and enjoyment of masters of coasting vessels. In 1890 this club moved to more comfortable premises on Whangpoo Road, where it provided comfortable rooms, for the use of members and their guests, facilities for refreshments and recreation, a billiard room, library, and reading rooms. The *Seamen's Mission*, as a missionary society of the Anglican Church, was opened in Shanghai in the early 1890s for the "practical and spiritual welfare of seafarers of all races and creeds." There was also a place in Shanghai, called *Toc H* **or** *Talbot House*, where the ex- soldiers were encouraged to mingle and make friends, ignoring the normal rules of officer ranks or status. The aim of the *Talbot House* was to "express its ideals of co-operation and friendship across the normal barriers that divide people."

Like every other important world city, Shanghai had several Masonic lodges. At the beginning, they were either English or Scottish. Probably the most important was the English *Northern Lodge*, established in 1849. It was the first and the last Masonic lodge in Shanghai. The last meeting of this Masonic Lodge was held in Shanghai in 1962 after which all members moved to Hong Kong. Masonry was well-developed and attracted a significant number of foreign men in Shanghai. Their favorite meeting place was the *Masonic Hall,* owned by three English lodges. The *Masonic Hall* also hosted non-British masons. It was used by American Masons until 1928, when they founded their own American Masonic Temple in the French Concession. Members of English lodges or Scottish lodges gave their assistance whenever possible to non-British masons. The German *Lodge Germania,* was founded and maintained with British support. [12]

Among the most active early British social institutions were the "four sisters societies": the *St. Andrew's, St. George's, St. Patrick's* and *St. David's* Societies. The *St. George's Society* organized grand and glamorous charity balls. Its golf team played traditional games with the golf team of the *St. Andrew's Society.*

The annual balls held by the *St. Andrew's Society* in the 1870s and 1880s were among the largest in Shanghai and famed for their glamour. The initial objectives were to assist needy Scottish residents in Shanghai, but in 1893 there was no call upon the Society for charity, which was "the sign of general prosperity of the Scottish community" in Shanghai.[13] The *St. David's Society* assisted needy Welsh in Shanghai during the First World War, organized many annual charity balls, and paid tribute on St. David's Day to Welshmen who had died during the First World War.

The *St. Patrick's Society* aimed to provide an association for members of the Irish community and their friends, to organize celebrations on St. Patrick's Day and other Irish festivals, and to assist Irish people in need. To achieve that, it arranged large charity receptions and balls. It organized one of the largest ever balls at the Carlton Hotel for more than 1,000 people in March 1927.[14]

In time, British associations and clubs covered all conceivable fields of activity and knowledge: missionary work, charity, women's interests, recreation, science, animal care, horticulture, and politics. Some of them were very politically and financially influential, even if they did not have a high public profile.

The Shanghai branch of the London-based *Royal Empire Society* was one such organization. Amongst the founding members of this society in London was the future British Prime Minister, Lord Salisbury. From its very beginning, this society was financed by Barclays Bank, the Sassoon family and Jardine Matheson company. These large business and political players also founded the Hong Kong Shanghai Bank, with large interests in trade and opium traffic. The objectives of the Royal Empire Society were to "preserve the unity of the accumulation of information regarding the resourses and development of all parts of Empire". It promoted investigation and discussion on Colonial subjects generally, in the style of a learned society. Members saw themselves as the "healthiest product of the imperialism" and "the farseeing men."[15]

The *Society for Diffusion of Useful Knowledge* was another very influential organization. It established its branch in Shanghai in 1873, in order to "introduce the western science to China".[16] Until the outbreak of the First World War, the British could also join the very influential *China Association*. This association first aimed to pursue a policy of cooperation with the British Foreign Office, but later used all its power to show that the British Government was failing to effectively represent British mercantile interests in China.

Children of some wealthier British parents were under the care of the *Ministering Children's League*. It was created "for children of the educated and wealthier classes - to train them in habits of unselfishness and thoughtfulness for ... their poorer brothers and sisters." The Pony Club provided children with quality riding lessons. The *Boy Scout Association of China* and the *Girl Guide* movement attracted many foreign boys and girls in old Shanghai.

We can look at Shanghai as an international city, but we can also look at it as a place where different nationalities rarely mixed with one another socially, unless they were from a similar background. All nationalities had their own associations, clubs and entertainment venues, most of them created using the British model. Chinese most often socialized and did business with people from their own native regions. Norwegian, Swedish, Danish and Finnish societies organized joint meetings and occasional parties (Nordisk fest). Likewise, there was an inter - Slavic solidarity in Shanghai. Portuguese clubs and associations had members only from Portugal. Britons socialized mostly with Britons and if they generally had close relations with another expatriate group, it was with the Americans.

In the nineteenth century, Britons and Americans were equal members or functionaries in many clubs and associations, such as in the: *Philharmonic Hall, Shanghai Choral Society,* the *Shanghai Literary and Debating Society,* the *Private Nurses' Association,* the *Quest Society,* the *Racket Club,* the *Shanghai Bowling Club,* the *Shanghai Golf Club,* the *Shanghai Race Club,* the *Royal Asiatic Society* and many others. However, the First World War threatened to change this friendly spirit. The British distrusted American motives for not entering the war and the American community became isolated. Some Americans could not obtain membership in British clubs. This led Americans to create their own venues. The *Chinese Anglo-American Friendship Association* was established in 1914, with the intention of showing that American sympathies were with the British, in spite of America's proclaimed neutrality. In spite of this effort, American segregation from the British was noticeable in all fields: American Masons established the new *Shanghai Lodge*; American businessmen established the *American Chamber of Commerce* and the *American Union of Commerce;* American women founded the *American Association of University Women* and the *Mother's Club*. American sport enthusiasts established the *Socony Football Club* and the *American Swimming Association*. During this period, Americans also founded their most important organization—the *American Club*.

The British community was diverse with all types of social categories. Back in the middle of the nineteenth century, poor and sick Britons were treated at the Seamen's Hospital. The medical fee was $1 for sailors and $1.50 for officers.[17] During the First World War, 15% of foreigners were completely dependent on charity works and many of them were British.[18] Some British establishments did not admit Jews as members—despite their British citizenship. British Jewish millionaire Victor Sassoon opened Ciro's night club, after he had been refused membership at the British *Country Club*. In response to being refused membership at the *Country Club*, other British Jews founded their own *Jewish Country Club*. There were, of course, also Britons who could not afford the high fees at some exclusive clubs.

Yet another division within the British community in Shanghai became very apparent in the 1920s—that between Shanghailanders (many of whom had never lived in Britian,) and the consular officials and British trade representatives who were in Shanghai temporarily, often working for London-based companies. Shanghailanders were sometimes accused by London businessmen of being opposed to any measures which would weaken their positions, and were called the "small Treaty Port people." For their part, Shanghailanders were afraid that the British Government would renounce their extraterritorial rights and for this reason they accused London representatives of treachery. Still, during wartime, Britons seemed to be prompt in showing inter-British solidarity. The first British war fund was created in 1854 in response to the Crimean War, by the British Consul R. Alcock. All British citizens took part in giving donations, but not all were equally generous. British businessman T. C. Baele donated the highest amount of $500. C. M. Donaldson, who was the grand master of Masonic *Provincial Grand Lodge of the Royal Order of Scotland* donated only $10.[19]

More than a half century later, many British men went to fight in the First World War, and those who stayed rearranged their activities in accordance with the war situation. During that time, the *British Chamber of Commerce* was pushed by the Municipal Council to employ more women, so that male employees could join the army. The First World War also led to the creation of many British war funds and charity organizations: the *Royal Flying Corps Hospital Fund*, the *Blue Cross Fund*, the *Star and Garter Fund*, the *British Flower Shops*, the *British Mother's Fund*, the *Prince of Wales Fund*, the *Queen Mary's Fund*, etc.

The most active was the *British Women's Work Association*. It collected donations, engaged in offering medical assistance and produced items needed by British soldiers and sailors. The organization functioned in all 24 treaty ports in China, with its headquarters in Shanghai. Its activities were regularly covered by the *North China Herald*, where it was said that this organization "will live so long as it is needed and is needed as long as the war lasts." However, it lasted one whole year after the war ended. By October 1919, it had collected a total of $423,452 (the *Shanghai Race Club* alone contributed $26,500). It had produced in total 1,620,760 articles (garments, bandages and surgical dressings.) Within its structure, there were a Sock Department, and a War Dressing and Boundary Department.[20] American women had a special branch within the *British Women's Work Association*, until October 1917. With the American entrance into the war, that branch dissolved and American women organized their own workshop. At the close of the war, King George V bestowed the honor of Dame on the president of the association, Lady de Sausmarez. The association finally closed in December 1919, when its members formed the *British Women's Memorial Fund*. This fund was devoted to the welfare and needs of wives and children of British soldiers and officers.[21]

Once the war was over, the British community was quick to find new opportunities for social engagements. British women established the *British Women's Association*. This association organized parties, classes and lessons every day except weekends, for an annual membership fee of $6. It arranged needlecraft lessons, hospital aid and badminton tournaments. Each Friday at 5.30 p.m, members could attend screenings at the cinema.[22] The polo players founded clubs *A, B, C* and *D*. Several specific organizations were also established, such as the *Old Carthusian Society*, the *Old Tauntonian Society* and the *Old Westonians*.

In 1927 the outbreak of conflict between nationalists and Communists in China caused international concern about the safety of the European population in Shanghai. Subsequently, Great Britain dispatched a substantial force after 1928 and its presence soon led to the creation of some new football clubs. The *Wiltshire Regiment Sport Club* won the Football championship in 1930. The *Bedfordshire and Hertfordshire Regiment* came to Shanghai from Malta in 1927, and upon their arrival, they immediately established a football team. They turned out to be the best players, winning the cup in 1928. Another club, the *Lincolnshire Regiment Football Team* played in the Shanghai League and won the championship in 1932.

British sailors and navy officers opened the *Union Jack Club,* which had a billiard room, space for an orchestra and small apartments for general use. There was no entry fee or subscription. The cost of a bed was 10 cents. It was open all day long, but the bar closed after midnight and lights went out at 1a.m.. Due to the outbreak of the Second World War and departure of the British Navy from Shanghai, this club closed. The British Commander in China, Vice-Admiral Geoffrey Layton, on hearing about the closure announced: "it is with deep regret that I learned of the decision to close the *Union Jack Club*...The *Union Jack Club* filled a big need. It meant much to Services and the amenities provided by the club gave naval men a Home where they could spend their shore leave happily and safely without being exposed to the many temptations for which the great City of Shanghai is famous." [23]

There appeared several British war veteran associations. The *United Services' Association* was established as an organization of British ex-soldiers and officers. From 1918 until 1920, it helped 30 of its members to find accommodation and 30 other members to find employment. In March 1920, this association welcomed into its membership women who had served in the First World War in the United Kingdom or any other theatre of war. It thus became one of the few British organizations which opened their doors to women. Victor Sassoon established the *Royal Air Force Association,* in order to keep former squadrons and unit members in touch with each other. The *South African War Veterans Society* was another war-veteran association. It held annual dinners at the *Masonic Club*. It had 32 members in 1932, but only 19 remained in 1937.[24]

The late 1920s witnessed the creation of several extreme anti-Communist organizations such as the *Constitutional Defense League* and the *Shanghai Fascists*. They were established to support the authorities in the International Settlement "in the present crisis, and to act in the interests of the entire community."

Some smaller British clubs and associations appeared in the 1920s and 1930s, such as the *Victoria Club,* the *London University Society, Caldbeck's Club,* the *Girls' Friendly Society,* the *Royal Humane Society* ,the *British Returned Students Union* ,the *Unemployed Men's Club,* etc.

For instance, the *Unemployed Men's Club* came into being as a result of a letter written in the *North China Daily News* by J. R. Johnstone in October 1935. Mr. J. R. Johnstone invited all interested to form an association of educated British and American unemployed. Membership was restricted to "men of good standing only," who were at least years old and had been in China for over a year. After certain preliminary meetings, the association got under way. Out of a total 106 registered British men in 1936, only 39 were still unemployed in February 1937. Out of Americans, 8 were still unemployed during the same period of time.

Four London-based engineering societies were also active during the 1930s: the *Royal Engineers Old Comrades' Association,* the *Institution of Mechanical Engineers,* the *Institution of Civil Engineers (ICE)* and the *Institution of Electrical Engineers.*

Surely the most important British organization in the 1930s was the *British Residents Association (BRA)*. Its goal was to campaign against the "treachery" of the British Foreign Office, represent Shanghailanders' interests against the Shanghai Municipal Council and lobby against reform of extraterritoriality. It changed its objectives due to the war, and in 1939 became mostly a charity organization. In 1941 it became, with its 3,400 members, the largest British organization in Shanghai. It was also one of those rare organizations that included women in its membership.[25]

The outbreak of the Second World War in Europe mobilized the British population in Shanghai to establish the

Central War Fund, which had collected a total of $3,720,000 by 8 December 1941. Under British guidance, the *Allied Federation of Shanghai* was formed at the *Shanghai Club* in May 1941. This association expressed the united interests of British, Belgian, Czechoslovakian, Norwegian, Greek, Polish, Netherlandish, and Yugoslav nationalities in Shanghai during the Second World War. At the opening ceremony it sent the following letter to the British Ambassador Archibald Clark Kerr in Chunking: "The non-British members of the newly created *Allied Federation of Shanghai* want to express to Your Excellency their complete faith in the ultimate British and Allied victory in defending of the common cause of freedom and decency." They also expressed their hopes that similar associations would form throughout the Far East.

Once again, many young British men joined the army. The president of the *Zero Club*, Anton Piercy, organized in April 1941 a party for a group of British volunteers. For most of them, this was the first opportunity to go back home. British women once again mobilized to assist war efforts.

Soon after that, the Japanese occupation caused the closure of almost all British associations. Only a few remained legally active. The *British Residents Association* continued to exist, but it had to deal with the changed order in the city, where the former rulers became victims of Japanese repression.

For a long time, Chinese and British did not socialize much with each other, but during the 1930s the situation started to change - the more affluent Chinese were invited to parties and receptions, and ladies invited each other to luncheons. The British- dominated *Union Club*, was among the first to agitate for friendly cooperation between the foreigners and the Chinese. Several other organizations (e.g the *Sino-British Wu-Si Country Club* and the *Sino – British Cultural Association)* were also founded in order to show how the British and Chinese could and should socialize with each other. Many high ranked Britons married Chinese or White Russian women, even if this also meant their exclusion from the British jet set.

Most of the British associations were reestablished after 1945, but they needed then to cope with lost extraterritorial rights and the civil war between the Communists and the Kuomintang. It became also obvious that British firms could not compete with more energetic American entrepreneurs. This all clearly indicated that the golden time of British presence in Shanghai could not be revived. Finally, it ended with 1949. However, this end was not abrupt. The *British Residents Association* continued to work for several more years, and held its 15th annual general meeting in 1951. The notorious *Shanghai Club* existed for some years after 1949, giving women the opportunity of membership for the first time.. By the early 1950s, foreigners could not legally open associations and clubs any more.

In 1957, the last British firms, except the Shell Company, were forced to close their doors. The few foreigners who were still in Shanghai met at the *International Seamen's Club*, founded as a social establishment for foreign sailors, in the building of the former *Shanghai Club*. In 1959, there were fewer than 100 Westerners in Shanghai, of whom 53 were British. In the early 1960s there were around 30 foreign residents in Shanghai, mostly Britons, Danes, and Swedes. They met for a drink or lunch in a place they called the *Royal Air Force Club*.[26] They talked about the golden age of old Shanghai – a time that was never to be revived.

Endnotes

1. For the early activities of the *London Missionary Society* in Shanghai see the following articles in the *North China Herald:*, "Notes of a Traveler", October 19, 1850; "Notice", February 15, 1851; "Notice, Protestant Mission," 9 September 1854; "Notice", 9 August 1851; "Falling of the roof of Trinity Church," 24 June 1850.
2. "Shanghai Cricket Club," *North China Daily News* , 29 October, 1874.
3. For the *Shanghai Cricket Club:* See the following articles in the *North China Herald:* "Summery of News," 2 April 1874; "Shanghai Cricket Club," 10 January, 1893; 3 October 1878; also "Shanghai Cricket Club," *North China Daily News,*1874; *The North China Desk Hong List for 1886, 1909, 1915, 1916, 1918, 1919, 1920, 1924, 1933,*

1938; *China Press*, 6 May, 1931; *Municipal Gazette*, Volume XXXIII, 1939; *Shanghai Times*, 1 May, 1941.
4. *North China Daily News*, 10 March, 1938; *Shanghai Paper Club* (Shanghai, 1890); Harriet Sergeant, *Shanghai*, p. 34; Edward Denison, Guang Yu Ren, *Building Shanghai*, p. 68.
5. *North China Herald*, 16 February 1893; 30 March 1893; *North China Daily News*, 3 January 1889.
6. *North China Herald*, "Native Race," 19 May 1855.
7. For the Shanghai Rowing Club in old Shanghai see: *North China Herald*, "The Shanghai Rowing Club," 26 March 1874; 4 April 1878; 14 April 1893; 24 July 1920; 28 July 1920; 10 March 1937; 7 July 1937.
8. Hibbard, Peter, *The Bund, Shanghai, China Faces West* (Hong Kong: Odyssey, 2007) 323.
9. *Catalogue of the Non-fictional books in the Library of the Shanghai Club to 1 October*, 1932.
10
11. *North China Herald*, 17. March 1860.
12. The list of Masonic lodges in old Shanghai includes: *Northern Lodge* - The first Masonic Lodge established in Shanghai (in 1849); *Zion Chapter* – The Royal Arch Freemasonry, which functioned as a chapter of the *Northern Lodge* after 1861; *Shanghai Commandery U.D. Knights Temple* – The first Knight Templar Masonic Lodge, first called Celestial Encampment, whose charter dated back to 3 October 1862; *Shanghai Preceptory and Priory (Knight Templar)* – established in Shanghai on 3 October 1862; *Sussex Lodge* – the oldest Masonic Lodge in China founded in Hong Kong on 3 April 1845 and opened in Shanghai in 1863; *Lodge of Assiduity* – one of the earliest Masonic Lodges in Shanghai, formed the same day (in 1863) as the Sussex Lodge was resuscitated; *Tuscan Lodge* – English Lodge, founded in Shanghai in 1864; *Ancient Landmark Lodge* – known as "Mother Lodge" of the American freemasons in China, founded on 14 December 1864; *Lodge Cosmopolitan* – Scottish Lodge, granted the warrant on 7 March 1864; *Lodge St Andrew in the Far East* – Scottish Lodge, founded in 1864; *Provincial Grand*

Lodge of the Royal Order of Scotland – founded on 10 August 1865; *Cathay Rose Croix* – Founded in 1869; *St. Andrew in the Far East* - Scottish Lodge, established in 1871; *Lodge Germania* – German Lodge, founded in 1872; *Ancient and Accepted Rite of Freemasonry* – The higher degree of American freemasonry, organized its branches in Shanghai on 19 September 1901; *Lodge Saltoun* – Scottish Lodge, founded on 23 December 1902; *Sinim Lodge* – American Lodge, founded on 28 January 1904; *Oriental Lodge of Mark Master Masons* – English Lodge, founded in 1912; *Shanghai Lodge* – American Lodge, founded in 14 September 1914; *Lodge Erin (No. 463)* – Irish Lodge, founded in 1919; *Doric Lodge* – English Lodge, formed in Chinkiang in 1873 and removed to Shanghai in 1927; *Tuscan Chapter* – English Masonic Chapter, founded in 1931; *Amity Lodge* – Masonic Lodge under Filipino Constitution, established on 27 January 1931; *Lodge Shanghai Kilwinning* – Scottish Masonic Lodge opened on 24 June 1932; *Johannislodge Lux Orientis (Grand Lodge of Vienna)* - the consecration ceremony of this German lodge was held on 15 January 1933.

13. *North China Herald,* "St. Andrew Society," 20 October 1893.
14. *Shanghai Times,* 27 April 1927.
15. *North China Herald,* "Royal Empire Society," 3 February 1937.
16. *The North China Daily News,* The Annual Report, 29 January 1874.
17. *North China Herald,* "Seamen's Hospital," 5 August 1854.
18. *North China Herald,* "Shanghai's Poor," January 13, 1917; "War Funds," 6 January 1917.
19. *North China Herald,* Circular, 24 February 1855.
20. *North China Herald,* "British Women's Work," 6 October 1917; 13 March 1920.
21. *North China Herald,* 13 March 1920; 22 May 1920.
22. *Shanghai Times,* "The Woman Page," 5 February 1935.
23. *North China Herald,* 10 January 1920; 2 April 1940; 5 May 1930;

24. The list of the members includes: E. B. Macnaghten, G. H. Parkes, W. C. Divers, W. J. Taylor, R. T. Burch, H. Tobias, W. C. Woodfield, David Fraser, A. E. Jones, P. Tilley, J. H. Richards, J. C. Burgess, E. J. Daniels, J. C. Burgess, H. Bars and L. E. Canning.
25. For BRA See: *Foreign Office Files for China, 1949-1976*, Public Record Office Classes Fo 371 and FCO 21; *Dollar Directory*, January 1935; *Time*, "The Long Decade," 8 June 1959; *The North China Desk Hong List 1933, 1934, 1938, 1941; North China Herald*, 23 April 1941; *CICR*, 1941-46; Robert Bickers, "Changing Shanghai's "Mind,":" Publicity, Reform and the British in Shanghai, 1928-1931," lecture given at a meeting of the China Society on 20 March, 1991, Occasional Papers, 1992; Bernard Wasserstein, *Secret War in Shanghai*, p. 128; George F. Nellist, *Men of Shanghai and North China*, p. 11; Bernice Archer, *Internment of Western Civilians under the Japanese 1941-194,: A Patchwork of Internment*, (London: F. Cass, 1996) p. 81.
26. Gerald Clark, *Impatient Giant: Red China Today* (, New York: D. McKay Co., 1959) 121.

'MEMENTO GLORY'
Yang Jing in the context of her time and beyond
Emily de Wolfe Pettit

Transcience of human existence, obsession with beauty, luxury of material possession and subtle references to mortality: one could be speaking of Vanitas art of 17th century Holland and the associated memento mori. Yet these are subjects found with increasing regularity in new work of artists, and particularly female artists, living in 21st century China, either through the narrative of their works and or the fragility of the media employed; one of the most notable exponents being the Beijing born, raised and trained artist Yang Jing.

If one is prepared to move in time and space, striking similarities between these two contexts for the resulting dialogue in their visual artistic practices can be made and projections in determining possible future developments take shape. The background to the 17th century movement of Vanitas and its particular flourishing in Holland (or The Netherlands) was a society that had just undergone huge upheaval through the North European Reformation, ousted the Catholic overlords and embraced Protestantism housed in severe, unadorned churches, witnessing a dramatic decline and indeed prohibition of some forms of religious art. The usual sources of patronage –the Church and aristocracy – were superseded by an increasingly prosperous middle class, whose insatiability for acquiring and displaying art (even a local eatery would be adorned with delicately rendered works) lead to the burgeoning of a range of genres, most notably large-scale landscapes and emblematic still lifes, such as vanitas that befitted the pious and hardworking Protestant aesthetic. Though their outlook mellowed as their security increased and their wealth grew, these Dutch burghers of the seventeenth century never accepted the full Baroque style which held sway in the south and throughout Catholic Europe..

Now to tracing artistic developments in China and the

effects of an ongoing era of revolutions. Just as Northern Europe witnessed tremendous socio-economic and cultural upheavals through the Reformation, post-Cultural Revolution China continues to do so through burgeoning capitalism, urbanisation and massive population movements all of which arose from the well-known reforms initiated by Deng Xiaoping. Where the 17th century Dutch school saw new artistic genres develop in a premeditated move away from dogmatic and ideologically-centred art work, in China too there is arguably a deliberate departure now from the work characterised by references to political ideology of recent Chinese art history. While restrictions on art contentious in its political stance persist, the cause for departure from Mao's 'legacy' of Cynical Realism and Political Pop in the visual arts lies not so much in censorship, but in the now oversaturation of derivative references to Maoist iconography over the past decade. (Moreover, younger generations of Chinese artists do not have first-hand experience of such intervention in the production of their art, unlike their predecessors in the eighties or nineties). There is also a need for devices to navigate the profound uncertainty brought about by constant flux in contemporary China, and to survive it.

While social and political ideology and dogma have largely been the mainstay of male artists, it is female artists living and working in China today who have been most responsive in exploring the individual's personal plight in the ever changing context of modern-day China, often through a return to the quotidien. In the work of artists such as Yang Jing and her female friends and peers, elements of Vanitas in various forms gather pace: in the series 'A Piece of Life', Liang Yuanwei emphasizes processes rather than outcomes, with emphasis on the rendering of textures, colours and particularly forms, to the point that the search for solidity is deliberately undermined through her sobering repetition of domestic, old-world patterns – or to a different mind's eyes, a re examination of beauty through morbidity and the finite; Song Kun's protagonist 'Xi Jia', whose personal journey addressing a kaleidoscope of human emotional experience, shows her through the delicate agency of graphite drawing on diaphanous surfaces and an array of fragile media, such as broken glass, cotton or antique baubles; and elsewhere, Yang Liu has dedicated herself to a body of work over the past two years in which the defining cornerstone is the motif of decaying books from which trees soar with the triumphant view of natural phenomenon over man-made artifice – and in which vanity lies not in the insatiable desire for earthly possessions, but in the possibility of attaining Reason.

The work to date of their contemporary Yang Jing (b. 1976), perhaps explores the thematic narrative of Vanitas most rigorously, traversing time and cultures, and moreover artistic styles, with beguiling ease. Her works are dotted with references to other periods with a morbid fascination with death – Gothic wallpaper and frames which echo Victorian England and reinforce the impression of a 17th century Dutch still-life sitting. In her 2006 work 'My Carnival', in homage to the 16th century French School of Fontainebleau painting, 'Gabrielle d'Estrées and one of her sisters', which now hangs in the Louvre, Yang Jing wished to make a direct reference to the hedonistic practices of the French artistocracy of the period, in which the definition of beauty has what would now be considered a morbid quality through the use of deathly-white face and body powder, false wigs and restrictions to natural movement through severe corsetry. Her mannequin figures are framed by subtle cues to death, decay and the passing of time: the peeling of wallpaper and miniature machines of war in 'Flying to the Southeast' (2005); the roll of the dice in 'The Lucky One' (2006), playing cards falling through the air in 'Seven Day Tour of Tian'anmen' (2008). The increasingly uncertain temporal and spatial existence in contemporary China and the preservation of its culture are recurring themes of Yang Jing's work: in her 2004 'The Disappearing Pagoda' and the series 'Critical Point' (2006), 'TMCN' (2006) and 'Secret Fragrance' (2008), each present a heightened sense of physicality and sources of life (and cultural) energy, the first depicting the ancient practice of acupuncture, this holistic treatment seemingly defended by mannequins bearing weaponry, the latter presenting traditional Chinese landscapes painted on the mannequins' bodies, as if cultural practices are embedded in the person. Speaking with the artist, Yang Jing extols the features of her exquisitely crafted Japanese bakelite doll, the "Super Dollfie" (also a cartoon character), with human hair that she has used as her model for over the past two years and what drew her to this particular doll: the melancholia in its eyes. She continues: 'dolls are representative of wider cultural or social mores. The dolls I played with as a child in China were lacking any 'life-like' qualities, their most characteristic feature being their round base, *so they would never fall over'*. Mannequins, in themselves, lifeless, are the literal embodiment of Vanitas (its Latin definition is "emptiness"). Requiring a fantasy life to be created around them by children in play, they take on life-like qualities and do, indeed 'fall over' in Yang Jing's paintings. In 'The Lucky One' blood seeps from the dismembered legs of one such figure – making earthly pleasures in this work, a pack of Lucky Strike cigarettes, a brightly coloured stuffed toy and a bottle of Poison perfume, appear somehow complicit in death.

While Yang Jing addresses the reality of a highly material and fast-paced life in her earlier works through hedonistic escapism and a triumphant carpe diem (if not reckless) approach, in her new 2008 works "Fu Lu Shou", ('Good Fortune', 'Prosperity' and 'Longevity'), the artist takes a more subdued, cautionary approach with a notion of moral judgement now infiltrating this body of work. Here she explores the auspicious Chinese symbols that are so influential and enduring in everyday Chinese attitudes to life, fate and death through their associated emblems, all depicted on a stage set complete with curtains drawn and under artificially bright lights: the theatre of life, if you will. Good fortune, its character "fu" painted on a floating zeppelin and a junk boat carries the message "Yi Fan Feng Shun", meaning "Safe Journey", is also symbolically captured by peony flowers. In another corner, mahjong, the traditional game of leisure, normally involving gambling, shows a winning set. Yet there is also a moral warning to wordly excesses: here a lotus flower, traditionally symbolizing purity and a noble character in Chinese moral fables. Likewise, in the stage set of "Lu", (prosperity), Yang Jing paints a small skull in a considered point to "remind that we should not only think about making material wealth; one can be destroyed if greedy. It is spiritual wealth that cannot be taken away in death". Finally, in 'Longevity', the artist makes a striking take on the concept "Long live Chairman Mao": beyond symbolizing longevity, Mao here, as in the lives of many people throughout China and still today, actually achieves something closer to immortality, embodied again in his little red book. The fascination with immortality is of course not new in China: the ancient and still popular use of ginseng, traditionally thought to provide immortality, appears in this painting, as does a peach fruit, a gift older Chinese people will receive at their birthday, according to the custom of wishing longevity. In each of the three paintings, a mannequin holds each of three puppets, the gods for "Fu", "Lu" and "Shou". In the words of the artist: "These three paintings tell us that we always hope for the best "Fu Lu Shou" in our lives and try everything to pursue them. However, sometimes life is out of our own control and full of coincidences, difficulties and the unexpected. People all have their different fates, like drama on a stage: this makes our life colourful and the mannequins here enact the unexpected or uncontrollable power in our lives".

It is doubtful Vanitas would have become popular if the Reformation and a strict Protestant aesthetic had not sewn the seeds for its development. Similarly, as our world is just embarking upon a new brand of re-formation – China arguably the key player in forming new systems – there is a predictable desire for artistic production that explores truly innovative integrations between Eastern and Western philosophy, epochs and artistic styles. The future audience for contemporary art in China, its young and burgeoning middle-class, will predictably hold a place for decadence in its art, at times meeting with the Cyberpunk trend of anime and film, at times a more contemplative return to essential questions of the individual's existence. Parallel to this, artistic creation amongst Yang Jing and her peers of post-Cultural Revolution artists would arguably not be taking the course of introspective self-examination if this generation did come from a background of predominantly only children and nuclear families, removed from immediate political infiltration into the everyday. Furthermore, while this generation may have become accustomed to some material comfort at this stage in a wave of capitalism and opening up to the West, conversation with the more reflective, such as Yang Jing, reveals that beyond serving an immediate purpose of gratification, such material, 'vanity' possessions are of not such great comfort as would warrant the bombardment of such imagery in everyday life. Her works are celebratory, but also cautionary tales as we see an artist mature, at once unveiling a unique, inward perspective, particular to many of the brightest lights amongst her contemporaries of female artists, and drawing great richness from several cultural points of view. Likewise, the viewer is asked to draw upon more than one cultural perspective in any possible deciphering of Yang Jing's conceptual world: indeed it is requisite to a new chapter of pluralistic work that seeks to lucidate the very purpose and direction of a fast-changing, material existence in its extreme.

SUSAN SONTAG'S "PROJECT FOR A TRIP TO CHINA"

JANET ROBERTS

REFLECTIONS ON MEETINGS WITH SUSAN SONTAG
I came to China in 2005,as a translation editor for Susan Sontag's *"Under the Sign of Saturn"* (2006). Her work was being translated into Chinese by Yao Jun Wei at Nanjing Normal University and subsequently was published by Shanghai foreign Language Press. Susan Sontag died during the edit, when Yao Jun Wei was a visiting professor at the University of Pennsylvania in Philadelphia, where I was a member of the faculty and on the Board of Directors of the Pearl S Buck Foundation. The task was given to me, as I was familiar with Susan Sontag's whole literary canon, and had met the illustrious intellectual and author several times in Manhattan, when she was accompanied by her son – journalist, David Reiff. Sontag's husband, Philip Reiff, taught at the University of Pennsylvania.

I, etcetera **(1978)**, is the title of a collection of Susan Sontag's short stories. In its preface is a quote by Sontag, from Nietzsche: *"What doesn't kill me makes me stronger."* One narrative is entitled *"Project for a Trip to China"*, and is based on the facts of her little known family history. Her father, a fur trader, travelled oftentimes to China, and died of tuberculosis, and is buried in China. Sontag says that when she was a child, one of the most amusing things she remembers was telling people that she had been born in China. Her birthplace was not China.

I have excerpted phrases and one line or two from each chapter to illustrate the threads of her contemplation about a trip to China.

I have always wanted to go to China.
i. Archaeology of longings
ii. Missionaries, foreign military advisors. Fur traders in the Gobi Desert, among my young father.

III have always thought: China is as far as anyone can go. Still true.

•

IV A trip into the history of my family. I've been told that the Chinese are pleased when they learn that a visitor from Europe or America has some link with prewar China. Objection: My parents were on the wrong side. Amiable, sophisticated Chinese reply: But all foreigners who lived in China at that time were on the wrong side.

V. I am interested in wisdom. I am interested in walls. China famous for both.

VII. Three things I've promised myself for twenty years that I would do before I die. – Climb the Matterhorn – learn to play the harpsichord – study Chinese.

IX. It is not that I am afraid of getting simple by going to China. The truth is simple....However, to be good one must be simpler. Simpler, as in a return to origins. Simpler, as in a great forgetting.

XI. Somehow, my father had gotten left behind in Tensing. It became even more important to have been conceived in China.

XII. Mythical voyage. The result is, inevitably, literature. More than it is knowledge.

XII. Perhaps I will write the book about my trip to China before I go.

Sontag's son, David Reiff, recently quoted "Project for a Trip to China" in his preface to a posthumous collection of essays, entitled *AT THE SAME TIME*. Essays and Speeches. Susan Sontag never travelled to China. She did not write the book about China. She died in New York City at the age of 71 years, in 2004. She certainly would have made that journey, if she had lived into the 21st century. She would be comforted by the fact that her books in translation, which outlive her are read in China.

–by Janet Roberts

Susan Sontag is known for the pathbreaking collection

of essays, "Against Interpretation"(1966), as well as for "*Under the Sign of Saturn*". Sontag's book *ON HANOI* (1968) was written as a protest against the Viet Nam War. She also wrote four novels including *"The Volcano Lover"(1992)* and *"In America(2000)*, which won the National Book Award for Fiction, as well as a collection of stories, several plays, including one after Ibsen, and seven works of nonfiction, among the best known, *"Against Interpretation" (1966) "Styles of Radical Will" (1969), "On Photography" (1977), Illness as Metaphor (1978)*, followed by *AIDS AS METAPHOR* which took on the subject of the marginalization of the sick and the impact of AIDS in America, and *"Regarding the Pain of Others"(2003)* She won several awards and national honors including the Jerusalem Prize (2001) and the Friedenspreis (Peace Prize) of the German Book Trade (2003). Susan Sontag was "something far more common in France than in the US: a public intellectual, a person with the right even the duty, to put forth ideas, as a contribution to the society's discussion of its life".

POETRY

Andrea Lingenfelter

Plane Trees, Spring and Fall (Hefei Nanlu)
you think as you cannot see
those walking beside me
are ghosts
plane trees rafting their leaves
in gutters flowing fast
they'll all have dropped
when I see them again and walk
beneath those bony arms
those ribs
sheltered from filtered light
a smattering of raindrops and smash
of tires in sooty puddles
the cables overhead crackling
not with news but with
the desire for light
same as the life that sleeps
inside these trees
each stippled body
each vessel of sun
green blooded and waiting

August-October 2006

SHANGHAI POEMS. BY THOMAS MCCARTHY

At Fudan University
Three girls who are as mad as hatters about Irish life,
Who studied Oscar Wilde, who sing *The Cranberries*,
Whose eyes are as blue as the sea off the Aran islands:
All approach the podium for a better glimpse of me,
Or not me, but the country that spoke to them
When I spoke. It is strange to come from the distant past;
To be too short-sighted for a full report,
To report upon a kind of music although tone deaf.
Now, I see all of China dancing, light-footed, expectant,
And clothed in denim. These girls toss the coinage
Of Shanghai at our feet, newly minted,
Twirling across the floor, brilliant, metallic.
I think of their grandfather, Mao, and their mother,
History, and how proud they must be – at this very moment –
To see the childhood of China grown curious, singing.

A Drunk Philosopher In Shanghai
While holding an Irish poet's kit-bag in the Patrick's Day
Parade, I try to remember last night's perfect Chinese meal.
My mind still holds an after-taste of Chinese cabbage:
I am thinking, also, of cured Irish bacon as I turn to greet

A drunken philosopher, here, in downtown Shanghai.
He has been travelling for days by buses and boats.
He heard that something was on, some big deal
Of a cultural thing; bloody *bodhrans*, fiddles and flutes.

He is reddened from drink; and his red emigrant's face
Sieves the sunlight of all its bleariness, of its spring rain.
Not a word of Chinese but God's affable lexicon
Has transported him across a thousand foreign miles. I claim
Him as a fellow citizen, and proud I am –
To hell with everyone – of this miraculous leprechaun.
Drunk, he has opened his head to the whole world;
And Shanghai opens, world-weary, to its latest citizen.

Our Second Visit to Shanghai

I study the fallen leaf. Not the vivid colour of the young
But time that swirls in its Chinese corner, time
That settles with all the depth of purple. It is death
That teaches her to be sensational, to be a mulberry tree;
To be silk with grief. I have been in love with this widow,
Mrs. Life,
Since the age of seven. Now her huge retrospective has opened

In the Expressionist Gallery downtown. It is an embarrassment
Of glass and steel, my love that could express itself
Like a studied, elderly poem. What is burnished and of age:
What has the wind and rain made of such an October roof?
A ruined greenhouse creaks in the dark. Tell me again,
Mrs. Life, about wisdom, about grapes with a coating of fur.

Here, it is time that has four hundred and eight names, the seasons
With thirty double names of the *Po chia hsing*. I prepare to meet life,
Thus attired with my well-earned *kuan ming*. Fully clothed,
I shall trespass like an indifferent, slightly drunk Irishman —

Though it is the fallen leaf that makes a report
To heaven, not any foreign ship at the Pagoda Anchorage.

Study, therefore, October falling in Shanghai and its remnants of ink,
Entire inky years unrolled slowly for sheer enjoyment;
The Shanghai highways, the glass and steel of phenomena
Here, therefore, is *Mrs, Life*, the palm plantations
Of the West River delta, the flow without enjambment —
That one sensational gallery, the poem, the widow *China*.

A Lute from Tung Tree Wood

After a poem from Liu Ji. (1311-1375) Zhejiang. A critic of
the Yuan Dynasty.

Gong Zhiquaio fashioned a lute
From tung tree wood.
When played, upon,
It made a beautiful sound
The best in the world.
He presented it to the official
In charge of rituals,
Who asked the court musicians
To examine it.
They said,
"It is not a precious ancient one."

One year later at home, Gong invited artists
To paint it, so that the texture looked old,
And seal carvers to carve ancient inscriptions on it.
Then he placed it in a box and buried it.
A nobleman bought it
For a hundred tael of gold,
And presented it at court.

All the court musicians praised it, saying,
"What a rare instrument!".

January, 2006. Nanjing. Janet Roberts.

BOOK REVIEWS

THEM AND US AND THEM
The Catalpa Series

Shirley Ganse, *Chinese Porcelain: An Export to the World* (2008)
Grace Lau, *Picturing the Chinese: Early Western Photographs and Postcards of China* (2008)
Lynn Pan, *Shanghai Style: Art and Design Between the Wars* (2008)
Frances Wood, *The Lure of China: Writers From Marco Polo to JG Ballard* (2009)
All - Joint Publishing (HK) Co. Ltd.

REVIEWED BY PAUL FRENCH

The Catalpa series essentially investigates from various angles the *"them and us"* question – the way Westerners have thought about, described and understood China both at home and while resident in the country. This history of interaction and curiosity is invariably currently understood – rather simplistically, by both sides – to have led to a raft of misunderstandings, racial stereotyping and long-running grievances. The West either "exoticised" China through everything from the repeated Chinoiserie crazes to the waxwork displays of concubines or demonized China and the Chinese courtesy of everything from Sax Rohmer's Yellow Peril Shilling Shockers or the newspaper's fears in the 1920s that West End flappers were being morally corrupted in Limehouse opium dens. It was, of course, the difference that appealed and determined so much of the image of China that reached the West whether the intricate patterns of the Chinese ceramics Shirley Ganse investigates or the Western fascination with postcards of rickshaws, footbinding, opium smoking and the various Chinese punishments (beheadings, cangues etc) that Grace Lau discusses. The same was generally true of the bestselling books about China, as Frances Wood shows. Difference is fascinating; similarity, dreary.

At the same time, the need to understand China was

deemed by Europe's statesmen as part of the 'furniture of empire'. More knowledge was needed – something recognised from the start of Britain's assertive push into China in the mid-nineteenth century . Thomas Babington Macaulay of the East India Company asked the House of Commons in 1840, *'What does anybody here know of China? Even those Europeans who have been in the Empire are almost as ignorant of it as the rest of us. Everything is covered by a veil, through which a glimpse of what is within may occasionally be caught, a glimpse just sufficient to set the imagination at work and more likely to mislead than to inform.'*

Meanwhile, the West that actually went to China sold opium to the weak-willed, Christianity to the heathen and generally interfered with the natural equilibrium of China, so the general thinking goes. The result has been that any discussion of the interaction between China and the West invariably ends with someone dragging up Kipling's endlessly repeated line:

'Oh, East is East, and West is West, and never the twain shall meet,'

Rarely do you hear the next three lines in which East and West do precisely that:

'Till Earth and Sky stand presently at God's great Judgment Seat;

But there is neither East nor West, Border, nor Breed, nor Birth,

When two strong men stand face to face,

Tho' they come from the ends of the earth!'

China in the West, the West in China – let's take the former, first. Those Chinese goods that filtered into the West across the disjointed trade routes of land and sea pretty instantly enthralled the public – first the wealthy who could afford them and then the masses, as trade routes became more developed, and both an export market from China and a rampant copycat culture took hold. Let's be generous and call it imitation and inspiration rather than fraudulence and piracy which is, of course, nothing new and flowed both ways, historically. How extensive the movement of products was that influenced each side's way of thinking and assumptions is incredible to ponder. In the 1780s, the Panchem Lama in Tibet already possessed a pair of European spectacles, a camera obscura that displayed views of London, while, to the surprise of a British delegation arriving in Tashichodzong in Bhutan, the local regent possessed a portrait of Lady Waldgrave, the Duchess of Gloucester, which he had on prominent display[1]. The Chinese Emperor's collection of mechanical toys and clocks from Europe are, of course, well known and are still on display in the Forbidden City. At the same time, wealthy Europeans had collections of Jingdezhen pottery while less wealthy Brits were admiring each other's "*Long Elizas*"[2].

Shirley Ganse's *Chinese Porcelain* shows that Europe was experiencing China through objects before it could even point to it on a map with much confidence while Grace Lau's *Picturing the Chinese* points out that, '*Even without direct contact, Westerners formed ideas about China and the Chinese from the prized wares and artefacts brought to Europe through exchanges of gifts and through trade.*' One wonders how honoured the Panchem Lama felt to receive a portrait of the Duchess of Gloucester?

The major point of this arrival of Chinese goods in Europe was that these imports soon inspired other manufacturers and quite soon products perceived by the general public as Chinese were actually far removed from the authentic originals – though they functioned perfectly well as mantelpiece ornaments. Thus, Chinoiserie was created and apparent everywhere, from the willow pattern china on English lower middle class Welsh dressers to aristocratic French jardins anglo-chinois – all of these fantastical Western visions of far off Cathay. Purists could claim that this locally produced Chinoiserie was all wrong. The Sir William Chambers-designed ten-storey pagoda at Kew Royal Botanical Gardens opened in 1762 at the height of Chambers' Chinoiserie period, though it was far from universally popular at the time. Horace Walpole, for one, who dabbled in Sinology, hated the pagoda, as did many

Sinologists who argued that pagodas should always have an odd number of floors[3]. But the public loved it as did they pretty much any Chinois exhibit. Londoners flocked to St James' Park in 1814 to see a pagoda perched on a brightly painted Chinese-style arched bridge spanning the canal. The pagoda unfortunately caught fire during the celebratory fireworks unveiling the whole project, so now it remains known to us only through Frederick Calvert's painting done just before the conflagration[4].

Walpole excepted, along side the European public seemingly cared little for the politics of the West and China's relationship – there was no serious outcry about the First Opium War – nor evinced overly much concern about the accuracy of any representation. They just would enjoy the exotic-ness of China. Charles Dickens, along with thousands of other Londoners, was a curious visitor to the genuine Chinese junk moored at Blackfriars Bridge from 1848, while Triestinos in the then Austro-Hungarian Empire queued up to see Signor Wünsch's Cabinetto Cinese displaying all manner of Chinoiserie for public display[5].

The investors behind the Thames junk, Signor Wünsch and Frederick Calvert all profited handsomely from western fascination with China though far less than did Madame Tussaud's Waxworks which first displayed a model of Commissioner Lin and his Favourite Consort (complete with bound feet) in the 1840s and then later a "typical" Limehouse opium den. That the British had flooded China with opium; that Commissioner Lin had dumped 20,000 chests of contraband opium in the sea only to then be blasted with English cannon for his trouble, and that opium dens were few and far apart in Limehouse mattered not a jot to the fascinated paying public on Baker Street. At the time, the masses had no hope of getting to see the Prince Regent's Royal Pavilion at Brighton where every room was decorated with Chinoiserie while Triestinos were not generally invited just up the road to Archduke Maximilian's Castle Miramar that also featured Chinese-inspired rooms.

And so as to the West in China...Frances Wood's

excellent and concise round up of western writers on China usefully reminds us that it's not just those that fell head over heels for China that need to be remembered. There are also those who just imagined China – among whom Wood would include Marco Polo (she is, of course, the author of the overtly sceptical *Did Marco Polo go to China?*)[6] and Sir John Mandeville who probably never ventured further than Calais, if he ever existed![7]). As with the fabulists and liars, Wood also notes that not all the serious writers about China were seduced. Of course, one can be lured to a train wreck as easily as anything else – it's the genuine fascination, not the in-depth appreciation that's important here. So while we have those who came to love China, we also have those who weren't so easily persuaded?

Indeed, criticism of China came quickly. As both Lau and Wood point out, it was only shortly after the Dutchman Johann Nieuhoff published his eyewitness sketches of China in the 1660s (the first semi-reliable images of China to appear in the West) that writers were criticizing China[8]. Both point to Daniel Defoe's little read follow up to Robinson Crusoe where his hero travels to China describing the people he finds as a *'contemptible herd'* and, *'a crowd of ignorant, sordid slaves.'*[9] Nieuhoff appeared in English in 1669; Defoe had Crusoe visiting and complaining about China – on the bookshelves in London by 1719.

Wood obviously rather likes the aesthetes who went to China, though notes that the problem with them, particularly the likes of Rene Leys and any number of the once prolific diplomat-scholars, was that whilst lyrical and passionate about China, they tended to look backwards, to yearn for earlier times and were rarely supportive of China's attempts to modernise and rarely, if ever, supported either the 1911 revolution or the later nationalist government. Nostalgia is, it seems, an essential element in much of the West's impressions of China – Lau notes that photographs taken in the 1870s were still popular as postcards in the 1900s despite being obviously anachronistic by then.

Indeed, one wonders what exactly the reading public of Europe and America could possibly have imagined about

China – given the comparisons, some travellers who visited sent back. Jules Verne compared Hong Kong to a Kent or Surrey town; Peter Fleming compared Chengde to Windsor and Oxford with Peking; Auden and Isherwood described the countryside around Guangzhou as reminiscent of the Severn Valley; while Joseph Needham compared wartime Chongqing to Torquay!! No wonder there was some confusion in the public's mind after two centuries of exotic Chinoiserie.

Yet did others really investigate and try to dig deeper? In *Picturing the Chinese,* Lau provides some very useful background on the early Western photographers in China such as Beato and Miller, whose images are very familiar as they are constantly reproduced. Most illuminating is her potted biography of John Thomson whose work provided a Western audience with the best images of China to date in the 1860s and '70s. Many will know Thomson's street scenes and portraits, but are unaware that along with these images, he left informed observations in copious notes. Also well known are the gouaches of people suffering from goitres and tumours painted by the Cantonese artist Lam Qua and commissioned by the medical missionary Peter Parker. Both the illustrations and Thomson's early photographs and notes offer us invaluable insights into nineteenth century Chinese life[10].

One book in the series, Lynn Pan's *...Shanghai Style*, is slightly different in that it looks at western ideas – in this case: typography, art and design – flowing into China to be adapted and reinterpreted between the wars. A flow of Chinese to the west for education and inspiration as well as a greater interaction in the relatively censorship-free treaty ports helped create a fusion that combined ideas and forms from the two cultures. This was one instance where East did meet West. The Haipai or Shanghai School led to a creative outburst in the arts that sought to create a progressive modernist avant garde specific to China. The Republican period between 1911 and 1949 saw a fusion of East and West in many sectors from the sciences to discussion of democracy as writers such as Frank Dikötter[11] have recently shown. Likewise, a growing number of

Chinese academics are also now recognising that both sectors drove the vibrancy and the cosmopolitan nature of Shanghai society, represented most clearly in the city's art and design of the period, whose influence extended across Republican China to differing degrees.[12] Them and us. Us and them? It's been a long and multi-faceted history, but there were clearly moments when, as Kipling might put it, the two stood "face to face".[13]

Endnotes

1. See, Kate Teltscher *The High Road to China*, London: Bloomsbury. 2006.
2. The English liked the long porcelain jars decorated with Chinese ladies that the Dutch called lange lijza, which the English promptly anglicised to "Long Elizas"
3. See Walpole's essay of 1780, *On Modern Gardening*
4. Calvert's *A View of the Chinese Bridge in St James' Park* was published by Burkitt & Hudson of Cheapside, London in 1814 and sold for 10s. 6d. a copy. The original is held in the King George III Topographical Collection at the British Library
5. A large sketch of Senor Wünsch's Cabinetto Cinese can be seen in Trieste's Museo d'Arte Orientale
6. Frances Wood *Did Marco Polo go to China?* London: Secker & Warburg.1995
7. Referring to Mandeville's Travels first published circa 1360s and now available in the Penguin Classics *The Travels of Sir John Mandeville*
8. Jan Nieuhoff (1669) An Embassy from the East India Company of the United Provinces to the Great Tartar Cham Emperor of China
9. Daniel Defoe (1719) *The Further Adventures of Robinson Crusoe*
10. By coincidence, both the bulk of Thomson's photographs of China and many of Lam Qua's paintings for Parker are housed in the Wellcome Collection in London
11. Frank Dikötter *The Age of Openness: China before Mao,* Hong Kong: Hong Kong University Press.2008.
12. China Daily, *The Top 10 Trends in Publishing*, 30 December, 2008.
13. Rudyard Kipling, *The Ballad of East and West,* first published 1889.

STAIRWAY TO HEAVEN
Stairway to Heaven: A Journey to the Summit of Mount Emei by James M. Hargett. Albany: State University of New York Press, 2006.

REVIEWED BY FRIEDERIKE ASSANDRI[1]

Stairway to Heaven is a study of Mount Emei in Sichuan, one of the four famous Buddhist Mountains of China. Taking a refreshingly new approach to the task of describing the complex cultural phenomenon of a Chinese famous mountain, the author proposes to "lead the reader on a trip to Mount Emei" (Hargett 3), following the detailed and fascinating travelogue of Fan Chengda, who climbed Mount Emei in 1177.

In addition to this central concern, the author attempts to examine the mountain as the "multifaceted phenomena of human experience" (Hargett 2), which constitutes a Chinese famous mountain. To this end, he examines five different ways in which human beings interacted with the mountain, namely: 1) myths about the mountain's religious origins; 2) legends of Daoist immortals associated with the mountain; 3) the arrival and development of Buddhism on the mountain; and 4) literary descriptions about Mount Emei and 5) tourist activity.

The introduction presents the study's methodology and describes ancient Chinese conceptions of mountains as well as the physical features of Mount Emei. In the subsequent chapters, the reader embarks on a 'journey', where translations from Fan Chengda's travelogue and other literary sources guide him through space and time, towards the summit of Mount Emei. Interwoven in this 'literary journey,' the author provides historical and analytical accounts of the history of the ancient state of Shu, its capital Chengdu, and Jiading County, where Mount Emei is located.

Supplemented with two maps and four pictures – the latter, unfortunately of poor quality s– the study takes the reader on the breathtaking climb, visiting monasteries and historical sights the way they presented themselves in the Song dynasty, all the while enjoying the natural scenery.

The chapter "The Summit" describes the climax of the ascent to Mount Emei with the apparition of the atmospheric light phenomenon called 'Buddha's glory', which Fan Chengda, like other pilgrims, perceived as a manifestation of the Bodhisattva Samantabhadra. Fan Chengda immortalized his experience in a poem to be carved in the rock as a *koan* ('public case')—a fascinating literary expression of a layman's experience of a state of spiritual 'awakening.'

The last two chapters of the book discuss the process of a mountain becoming a Buddhist mountain and the history of Emeishan through the Ming and Qing dynasties, and in the eras of the Republic and of Communist China.

The strong presence of Buddhism in the 'identity' of Mount Emei is a major theme throughout the book. Hargett argues that Mount Emei first became famous for natural beauty and association with Daoist saints, and only when this fame was firmly established, did the imperial government and local religious and political leaders forge the mountain's Buddhist "identity" to "sanctify and reconfigure" the space of the mountain (138).

Focusing on imperial patronage and on the process of legitimization of the mountain as a Buddhist mountain, Hargett describes the development of the "Founding Myth" (141), which served to establish the crucial link between Emei, Bodhisattva Samantabhadra, and the 'Buddha's glory' light phenomenon, as well as its scriptural authentication. Furthermore, the author discusses the important role of pilgrims, travelers and gazetteers in the development of the image of the mountain. A short overview of the "Big Picture" (160) of the development of the first three and eventually, four famous Buddhist mountains, completes the analysis.

The final chapter gives special attention to imperial patronage and the growing pilgrimage and tourist activities. With the vicissitudes of the twentieth century, the Buddhist theme re-emerges in the context of the tourist industry of a "modern, market-driven society" (192)— with a government sponsored gigantic statue of Samantabhadra, as big as the colossal Buddha of Leshan, built during the Tang dynasty.

In the introduction, the author pointed out the need to overcome 'sectarian' limitations' (7) in the study of complex cultural phenomena like famous mountains in China. While the discussion of Buddhist developments rests on solid foundations of historical and archeological evidence, the Daoist 'thread' in the fourth chapter somewhat neglects the historical dimension of Daoism and its texts. Except for a citation of the 3rd century *Baopuzi* (The Master who Embraces Simplicity, DZ 11852), Hargett discusses pre-Tang Daoism largely based on citations from the 11th century compilation *Yunji qiqian* (Cloudy Bookcase with Seven Labels, DZ 1032), which associate various deities and texts with Mount Emei. Hargett suggests that such tales of (seemingly random) associations of deities and saints with Mont Emei were part of a "mapping" process that helped to legitimize the mountain as a "full fledged Daoist mountain" (Hargett 73).

However, if instead of looking at the 11th century source, with the random associations of various deities and texts with the mountain, one chooses to limit the discussion of pre-Tang Daoism on Emeishan to pre-Tang textual sources, a different picture emerges. Pre-Tang sources are consistent in confirming what Hargett cited from the 3rd century text, namely that the Sovereign of Celestial Perfection transmitted a method of cultivation to the Yellow Emperor on Mount Emei.[3]

A 'spatial' approach in establishing the connection of particular methods of cultivation with definite places, like Mount Emei, could subsequently offer a promising line of research into the little-known early developments of Daoism, however this would require careful attention to the historical dimension of the sources used and extensive further research. For the moment it seems premature, to speak of Mount Emei as a "full-fledged Daoist Mountain."

Notwithstanding the problematic section on Daoism, the book is very commendable. The alternation of translations from literary sources and historical discussion combined with occasional accounts of the author's first hand experiences make for very pleasant and interesting reading. The vivid translations allow the reader to envision the sceneries, while historical and academic discussions complement this imaginative part with substantial information. Thus, the author has fully realized his scope to take the reader to a journey to Mount Emei.

Endnotes

1. An earlier version of this review was published in Journal of Song-Yuan Studies 37 (2007): 238-241.
2. DZ numbers refer to Schipper and Verellen: The Taoist Canon. A Historical Companion to the Daozang. Chicago: University of Chicago Press. 2004.
3. Different texts mention different names, yet overall there are consistencies: Zhengao (DZ 1016, 10/6b, 4-6):五斗內一 and 涓子內法. Tao Hongjing notes that "五斗" refers to "真一". Taishang lingbao wufu xu (DZ 388): 真一 (3/18), 三一 (3/17) and 五芽 (3/20). Ge Hong, Baopuzi 18 (DZ 1185): 真一, 守一, 守真一, and 三一. Qiyu xiuzhen dengpin tu (DZ 433): 五牙三一 . Jinque dijun sanyuan zhenyi jing (DZ 253): 守三一. Compare Raz, Gil. The Creation of Tradition: The Five Talismans of the Numinous Treasure and the Formation of Early Daoism. Diss. University of Indiana, Indiana, 2004, (244) about similarities in Baopuzi 18 and Taishang lingbao wufu xu: "It is clear that the two texts are based on similar content, an underlying teaching of the Three-Ones and the Perfected One, also named "Preserving the One," associated with the Yellow Thearch and the Luminary of Mt. Emei." Compare also Andersen, Poul. The Method of Holding the Three Ones. London: Curzon Press, 1980.

BRITISH RULE IN CHINA

British Rule in China: Law and Justice in Weihaiwei, 1898-1930, by Carol G S Tan. London: Wildy, Simmonds and Hill Publishing, 2008.

REVIEWED BY LIU WEI

Weihaiwei, a small coastal area of roughly 285 square miles in Shandong Province of Eastern China, almost equally distant from Beijing and Shanghai, came under British rule by leasehold for 32 years as part of Britain's effort to establish a naval base to counter-balance the ambitions of other European powers, especially Russia and Germany, in North China. Though there have been two narrative accounts of the colony's history (Pamela Atwell, *British Mandarins and Chinese Reformers: The British Administration of Weihaiwei (1898-1930) and the Territory's Return to Chinese Rule, Oxford University Press, 1985;* Zhang Jianguo and Zhang Yongjun, *Weihaiwei under British Rule,* Shandong Pictorial Publishing House, 2006), Dr Tan's is the first panoramic study of the territory from a legalist's perspective, and therefore sheds lights on some previously scarcely touched areas regarding the British administration's achievements and failures such as criminal and civil justice and the headmen mechanism.

Nicknamed "The Cinderella of the Empire" against its glorious sister Hong Kong ("the Pearl of the East"), Wei-hai-wei, or Fort Weihai, hardly ever claimed public attention as a British colony in China. Its usefulness to the British was constantly questioned even then. One of the few recent academic works in English literature on the subject regards the decision to occupy the territory as a result of " the irrationality of empire" (Clarence B. Davis, Robert J. Gowen, "The British at Weihaiwei: A Case Study of the Irrationality of Empire, *The Historian,* Vol. 63, 2000). According to Reginald Johnston, the territory's last commissioner, British prestige had not been advanced by the occupation of Weihaiwei, as compared unfavourably with the progress made by the Germans and the Japanese in their respective colonies of Kiaochou (Jiaozhou) and Dairen (Dalian) in the neighbouring areas. Much of the reason for the failure to turn the colony into a "Second Hong Kong" was due to the uncertainty of the duration of the lease together with its legal status. The slowness on the British part to take control of the territory in the two years immediately after the signing of the Peking Convention was accompanied by the confusion over jurisdiction and applicable law, which court or courts had jurisdiction over criminal and civil cases and what law was to be applied, as Dr Tan points out. The questions were only answered later in practice: the office of the magistrate would deal with most of the cases, whether criminal or civil, using English law when non-Chinese subjects were involved, and Chinese law as far as was reasonable and just when Chinese subjects were involved, while others, mostly minor cases, were left in the hands of village headmen applying Chinese customs. Some effort is made to debate on the question of sovereignty regarding territories like Weihaiwei, but it only seems to be of academic interest because 'jurisdiction without sovereignty did not have any consequences for the system of law' (p258) and, according to Oppenheim, lease is just disguised cession, because sovereignty is considered 'absolute'. This matches the Chinese reflection, both official and popular, on the lease of Weihaiwei as relinquishment of Chinese sovereignty.

Few Chinese could pinpoint Weihaiwei on the map; fewer would connect it to the Chinese defeat in the first Sino-Japanese War of 1894-95, despite the famous Liugong Dao, a small island less than a mile off Weihaiwei that served as the Chinese imperial navy's main base during the war; still fewer were ever aware that Weihaiwei had been under foreign rule except for the Japanese occupation in the Second World War when the country's entire coastal line was lost to the enemy. Weihaiwei did not even take the nationalists' fancy then and now, who normally would seize every opportunity to stir things up. And unlike the Chinese inhabitants in British Hong Kong and the International Settlements of Shanghai, who from time to time rose to challenge the foreign rule, the populace of Weihaiwei who, after the violent resistance at the beginning, seemed mostly satisfied with their British masters' treatment, would occasionally try to move the marker stones of the border outwards, because outside the territory there were often civil wars and political turmoil, according to recent Chinese research (Wang Yiqiang, 'A Study of Weihaiwei's Legal System under British Rule', *Global Legal Review*, Beijing, Spring 2004,pp 66-74). This unforced collaboration from the Chinese subjects was largely the result of the British authorities' flexibility in exercising their jurisdiction, notably applying Chinese law and customs whenever and wherever possible, and using the village elite (headmen) as their connection with the common people, who receive considerable attention from Tan.

The headmen system was a legacy of the traditional Chinese imperial governance at the lowest level as an extension of the imperial bureaucracy, which ended at the county (or, in Weihaiwei's case, district) level. Among its major functions were book-keeping, tax-collecting and arbitrating. It drew its human resources from clan chiefs, wealthy villagers, or the educated elite (one other source may have been retired mandarins, as one of the village headmen posing for the camera in the book clearly bears the patch of the Eighth Rank on his robe, the rank of a lieutenant county magistrate, while headmen were caretakers outside the bureaucratic ranking system). Dr Tan does justice to the British magistrates, especially the two longest-serving commissioners James Lockhart and Reginald Johnston (the 'British Mandarins'), for their wisdom in incorporating Chinese customary law into the English legal practice (the cantonment of the magistrate was obviously drawn from the traditional of Justices of Peace at home but the applicable law in most cases it dealt with was Chinese, for instance). But to suggest Weihaiwei's uniqueness in this aspect would need further scrutiny. Recent scholarship on the social and political structure of Hong Kong's New Territories shows a similar incorporation of Chinese customary law and headmen system into the British colonial administration (G.E. Johnson, 'Leaders and Leadership in an expanding New Territories Town', *The China Quarterly*, No. 69 (March 1977), pp.109-125; James Hayes, *The Great difference: Hong Kong's New Territories and Its People, 1898-2004*, Hong Kong University Press, 2006; Su Yigong, *Chinese Law, Western Application: Traditional Chinese Law and Customs in Hong Kong*, Beijing, 2005). A comparative study of the two colonies would surely bear fruit. Work will also need to be done on the election mechanism of headmen and the precise division of jurisdiction between the British magistrate and the headman, which are not covered by Dr Tan's study, obviously for the lack of Chinese sources. One recent piece of research on the village headmen system in a neighbouring region (Huaiyin Li, Village Governance in North China, 1875-1936, Stanford University Press, 2005) may shed light on such areas, especially because, according to the author, the Chinese county magistrate also ruled differently in different cases according to different local customs even sentiments, amazingly similarly to the British practice in Weihaiwei.

CHINA CUCKOO

China Cuckoo by Mark Kitto. London:Constable and Robinson, Ltd., 2009.

REVIEWED BY TESS JOHNSTON

Caveat: I know Mark and I knew Moganshan long before Mark got there. And I like them both. Perhaps this has compromised my ability to review this book impartially. But I think I can still spot a bum book when I read one – and this is definitely *not* a bum book.

In fact, it is a remarkably fine book and one that I think the Brits call 'a thumping good read'. With the book's subtitle, *'How I lost a fortune and found a life in China'*, I was not expecting much history of Moganshan. After all, Mark had candidly admitted in his recent R.A.S. lecture that nothing much ever happened there. I thought we would get instead a great deal on how he lost his mini-media empire in China. What we get is a great deal of the former and just a bit of the latter. (But enough to know that this book will never be found in bookstores in China, alas.)

The story goes back to 1999 when Mark first meets Moganshan, almost predestined it would appear, a perfect match of man and mountain. From an unpromising first stay there with his Shanghai popsie in an unheated old villa with frozen pipes and no water (how *did* they manage that for three nights?) he is hooked. We wind up 350 pages later with Mark, wife, children, dog, car, villas (two) and a restaurant business up on the mountaintop. How he got from point A to point B is a narrative of perseverance, hardship and the ability to endure, indeed thrive – in other words, a typically Chinese story.

In this remarkable journey we get to know the man as well as the mountain. It's all there, a detailed and lively retelling of the history of Moganshan from its inception to its final abandonment little more than half a century later. And Mark is revealed as a Renaissance man, a Man Mountain Dean with a poetic soul (who can write a line like "I was away with the fairies" and get away with it). He can also hew wood, hike alone for days from mountaintop to mountaintop, drink his adversaries (and friends) under the table and, at the end, turn out typical English breakfasts (AKA 'Heart Attacks on a Plate') in a crowded kitchen of *The Lodge*. 'My poor long-suffering wife. She married a successful entrepreneur, a mini media mogul no less, and she had ended up with a cook.'

In his darkest days, of which there were many, I doubt if Mark could have known how well it would all turn out. He overcame incredible odds and won (most of) his battles again his adversaries, the obstructive and obnoxious petty bureaucrats who made his life miserable and his Moganshan tenure problematical. He fought the good fight and he prevailed. (Must be that stout English heart, or perhaps his tough Welsh Guards infantry training?) I, for one, was dazzled by what he accomplished.

Mark's writing style is easy and fluid, anecdotal and philosophical, filled with pathos and humor – in sum, everything you want to find in a book. He never hesitates to make fun of himself, to reveal his pratfalls, his failings, his fears, and as you follow him in his journey your admiration and affection for this modern-day Don Quixote grows. I found myself thinking over and over again, 'Gawd, I could never have done that.' And when I finished this very personal and beautifully-crafted book, I (who sometimes fancy myself a writer) could only say of Mark's *China Cuckoo*: A perfect melding of man, mountain, and chronicler.

WHITE SALT MOUNTAIN
White Salt Mountain: Words in Time by Peter Sanger.
Kentville, Nova Scotia: Gaspereau Press, 2005.
REVIEWED BY LINDSAY SHEN

White Salt Mountain is a chase across centuries and cultures. Defying categorization as biography, travelogue or literary criticism—though it does each with aplomb—it is foremost a meditation on the power of words to unite readers and writers across time and place. By Sanger's own admission, *White Salt Mountain* is a "mystery," that revolves around the allusions of its title. It's a mystery uniting two rather unlikely protagonists—Florence Ayscough (1875-1942,) Shanghailander, educator, and Royal Asiatic Society librarian; and John Thompson (1938-1976,) one of Canada's most influential and ground-breaking poets.

Sanger's introduction to Ayscough came, quite literally, through her own words, via her inscription on the flyleaf of a copy of *Fir Flower Tablets*—the compilation of classical Chinese poetry she translated with Amy Lowell and published in 1921. Intrigued by this little-known woman of Canadian heritage, Sanger set out to compile her biography, and is particularly illuminating on the Nova Scotian and New Brunswick chapters of Ayscough's life. A widely published poet and literary critic, Sanger offers an incisive analysis of the *Fir Flower* poems, comparing them to subsequent translations, as well as to the translation work Ayscough undertook without Lowell. The latter poem he finds elliptical, terse, fragmentary and Modernist—qualities to which, Sanger argues, John Thompson was very much attracted.

The correspondences Sanger draws between Ayscough's translations of Tu Fu and passages in Thompson's widely revered collection *Stilt Jack*, are convincing in themselves; however, Sanger's explanation of the mode of transmission poetically seals the argument. On retiring from Shanghai in 1923, Ayscough lived in New Brunswick, where she focused on the translations of Tu Fu that were to make up her two-volume Tu Fu "autobiography" published in 1929 and 1934. The University of Acadia in Nova Scotia, which had awarded Ayscough an Honorary D.Litt in 1927, has volume one (a gift from Ayscough,) but volume two has been replaced by a facsimile edition. Sanger conjectures that the missing volume was borrowed by Thompson, and was burnt in the fire that destroyed his New Brunswick farmhouse in 1974.

The interweaving of texts creates a lushly layered book that makes many demands of its readers as it telescopes between Tu Fu, Blake, Milton, Melville, Marlowe, Donne, and North American Indian stories. It reminds us that as humans, our literary traditions are a shared conversation that, like the eponymous White Salt Mountain, ties together locations and people as disparate as a mountain along the Yangtze, a sojourner in Shanghai, a New Brunswick poet, and us as their readers.

THE MAN WHO LOVED CHINA
The Man Who Loved China: The Fantastic Story of the Eccentric Scientist who Unlocked the Mysteries of the Middle Kingdom by Simon Winchester. New York:HarperCollins Publishers, Inc., 2008.

REVIEWED BY KIM TAYLOR

This is a riveting read of a book about an extra-ordinary man, Dr. Joseph Needham, CH, FRS, FBA, one time master of Gonville and Caius College, University of Cambridge, founder of the Needham Research Institute, Cambridge, and the man who conceived of the question 'Why did China, despite its countless scientific and technical innovations in ancient and medieval times, fail to have a modern scientific revolution and lead itself into modernity?' Needham was to spend the remaining two-thirds of his life in tireless, meticulous research trying to answer this question, and in so doing he gave the world *Science and Civilisation in China* which, including some posthumous publishing, so far reaches 24 volumes,

15,000 pages and 3 million words (p.9), one of the greatest feats of single author scholarship of all time.

The book manages to cover a lot of ground in only a 265 page read. Winchester masterfully and succinctly guides the reader through the peculiar, unorthodox upbringing of the young Needham; he dwells on Needham's many eccentricities and we learn that Needham had particularly leftist leanings and was very liberal minded, embracing nudism, outlandish morris dancing and radical church services. We romp through the outright success of Needham's early years at Cambridge where he read biochemistry and set out to explore the origins of life in the subject field of embryology. We are informed that he became a permanent Fellow of Gonville and Caius College at the ripe old age of 24 and in the same year he married fellow biochemist researcher Dorothy Moyle, setting himself up for a lifetime of scientific scholarship within the idyllic environs of Cambridge University. And then, by just page34, it is revealed that Needham's life was unexpectedly turned upside down by the arrival of a young Chinese biochemist, affiliated to his wife, who was to become his muse and lover.

Her name was Lu Gwei-djen (鲁桂珍), a budding scientist from Nanjing, China, who had been accepted as a researcher at the Needhams' lab in Cambridge. However her influence was to extend much further beyond Tennis Court Road and she was to open up a world of immense prospects and unchartered scholarship to a Needham who became simply fascinated, even obsessed, with China through her guidance.

This is a long, complicated story, and wonderfully brought to light through Winchester's illuminative, concise prose. China at this time was in the throes of a series of long and debilitating wars and science had had to flee to some of the remotest corners of the country. During a visit as the chief representative of the Sino-British Science Cooperation Office, Needham spent four years traversing the country from 1943-46, stumbling across one exiled scientific outpost after another in the most unlikely of places, meeting a number of resilient scientists, many of whom had studied abroad and who were overwhelmed by meeting this latter-day scientific evangelist whose mission it was to learn about their research and to arrange where possible for the delivery of precious, rare scientific materials and literature. Needham would later in life draw heavily on the connections he made in China during these turbulent times.

Joseph Needham eventually returned to Cambridge, via a stint in Paris, in 1948 and set about preparing a manuscript which he believed would be a couple of years' work, and around 700-900 pages long on the 'Science and Civilisation in China' "a book addressed to ... all educated people... who are interested in the history of science... in relation to the general history of civilisation..." (p.171) No small aim for a biochemist. There ensued a frenzy of hyperactive research from his small set of college rooms at Caius, and aided by his assistant Wang Ling and the ever faithful Lu Gwei-djen, Needham started to unravel the complexities of Chinese scientific and technological advances over the entirety of recorded history as no man, Western or Chinese, had done before. Before long the one volume spawned into four, and then seven, and then more.

It is a tribute to the English education system that such a work could ever have seen the light of day. Already established as a biochemist, Needham was free within the framework of his Fellowship to explore the frontiers of knowledge. However, few could have anticipated that he would switch subjects entirely to two subject areas, sinology and the history of science, in which he had no formal training whatsoever. There was bickering and discontent within the Fellows' ranks, but an agreement was reached with his department to free Needham from all teaching duties to allow him to devote himself entirely to the preparation of his manuscript.

Reading through Winchester's fervent text, one is reminded of an era gone by, of a simpler life without all the electronic distractions of life today, when a man and his typewriter could change the course of scholarship. The intellectual brilliance of Needham is formidable, his clarity of thought extra-ordinary, his ability to see beyond the minutiae of detail and grasp the significance of the wider picture awe-inspiring. This was a man who had taken onto his shoulders the enormous weight of a completely unresearched field of scholarship in an entirely alien language and culture with little or no encouragement or support and he had the unassailable ambition, firm faith and dogged determination to make it happen. His conviction and conciseness of word were such that, as Winchester noted, "His first script, was always his final draft." (p.179)

Winchester manages to delve into the complexities of the history of Chinese science for a brief moment (p.183-88), but only scratches the surface of the huge body of knowledge that Needham commanded. Obviously Winchester is writing for a general audience, supposedly not interested in obscure facts, although it would have been a welcome service to the subject area to shine some more light on the characters involved and the manner of the inventions. The controversial nature of Needham's research is also not mentioned; the fact was that he remained an outsider, never accepted into his University's Faculty of Oriental Studies or Department of the History and Philosophy of Science. Terrified that his library and work would be torn apart after his death, he refused to allow his Institute to become a part of the University and so it stands independent and isolated in the shadow of the Cambridge University Library. Unsurprisingly, Winchester also shies away from attempting to answer the Needham question, a conundrum that still awaits a suitably brave scholar to confront in the final volume of the series, should that ever be published.

What Winchester does well, though, is to bring to life very vividly the process of the making of the man, and to explain the significance of certain events, however minor, and both personal and professional, that marked key turning points in Needham's life. He enlivens the story with wonderful, often humorous, anecdotes, and while he might linger overmuch on the more sensational aspects of Needham's life, he has succeeded in giving us a well-rounded, in-depth, factually accurate read. The fact that this is the first full-length biography of this brilliant, complex genius of a man goes to show that this book has been too long in the coming.

POSTSCRIPT

I was fortunate enough to meet Joseph Needham himself during his penultimate year of life in 1994 in the hallowed halls of the Needham Research Institute, Cambridge. At the time a very junior MPhil student in the History of Chinese Medicine I remember watching with much awe as the elderly and ailing Dr. Needham was wheeled into the Reading Room. With regularity he would stretch a trembling arm across the table reaching for his favourite sweets and the most senior of scholars would leap up with great alacrity to unwrap them and feed them to him in the most sycophantic of ways. Joseph Needham has now long passed away and the Needham Research Institute is dedicated to continuing his labours. However it is a great shame that Needham in all his years at Cambridge never groomed a successor, someone invested with the same breadth and scope of knowledge as he and capable of taking on the project. Instead it is broken piecemeal into separate sections and farmed off to distant scholars with their own research agendas. Short-term grants enable foreign scholars to visit and make use of the vast resources of the Institute's Library, but there is no training for another generation of historians of Chinese science, and the corridors of the Needham Research Institute echo empty indeed.

It is noteworthy that while Joseph Needham is practically unknown in the West, except to an exclusive few familiar with his work and provenance. In China, the vast majority of educated people have heard of Needham's Chinese name Li Yuese (李约瑟), and he is revered in the way that only the Chinese can worship accomplished and venerable academics. I thought it telling that at Premier Wen Jiabao's recent lecture at Cambridge University on February 2nd, the University authorities were falling over themselves to emphasise Cambridge's strong links to China and the strongest link, despite the diversity and enduring nature of scholarship there, remains Joseph Needham. May his name and work long live on.

THE JACQUINOT SAFE ZONE
The Jacquinot Safe Zone, Wartime Refugees in Shanghai by Marcia R. Ristaino. Palo Alto: Stanford University Press, 2008.

REVIEWED BY LI TIANGANG

As a historian working on the history of Shanghai, and, as a native who was born in Shanghai, I knew nothing, not even the name of Father Robert Jacquinot who saved 300,000 Shanghainese during the first year of the Anti-Japanese War in 1937. The first time I heard about Fr. Jacquinot was in 1994 when a Canadian Ph. D. student John Meehan consulted me when he was investigating materials about the Jacquinot Safe Zone in Nanshi, Shanghai 1937.

Fr. Robert Jacquinot de Besange S. J. (1878-1946) was a heroic individual who convinced Japanese and Chinese armies to allow him to set up a safety zone to protect civilians in Nanshi (Nantao), south Shanghai from November 1937 to June 1940. 'The Shanghai Safety Zone (Shanghai *anquan qu*) brought security to 250,000-360,000 during the most chaotic and dangerous period of the undeclared war.' An effort was made to recreate the Shanghai safety zone in other cities like Nanjing, namely, by John Rabe. Becoming internationally known as 'the Jacquinot Zone' Jacquinot is acknowledged in the Geneva Convention of 1949 for his humanitarian contribution. Recently, the story of Jacquinot was researched and written about by historian, Dr. Marcia R. Ristaino, in her book *The Jacquinot Safe Zone, Wartime Refugees in Shanghai*.

Fr. Jacquinot originally came from France. Before his arrival in Shanghai as a Jesuit Father in 1913, he spent his early years in Belgium and in England learning the English language, as well as Latin and Greek. As a linguist, he took a position teaching English in Aurora University, Shanghai (today, Jiao Tong University). In Xu Jia Hui, it was easy for him to learn Chinese mandarin and Shanghai dialect. He became fluent in Chinese, French, English, and Japanese, all the languages required in Old Shanghai. He made a lot of friends in Shanghai when he started his charity works for Shanghainese during the war and great flood disaster rescues in 1931. Jacquinot spent a total of 27 years in Shanghai before returning to Paris in 1942. Fr. Robert Jacquinot de Besange should be a name we Shanghainese keep in our remembrance.

When the Anti-Japanese War of 1937 broke out in Shanghai, my father was seven years old, and lived in the Hongkou battlefield area from where his family had to flee as refugees. They crossed over the bridge on Soochou Creek to the Central International Settlement for safety. He told me many sad stories about the camps, but he did not mention Father Jacquinot's name. His name was not mentioned in my school's textbooks. When I was trained as a historian at Fudan University in the 1980s, I did not find Fr. Jacquinot's name nor any attention to his contribution. My classmates, colleagues and the students knew almost nothing about him. Likewise, Marcia Ristaino says Jacquinot's works 'were almost entirely unknown to American scholars, Chinese researchers, and even to most of the Jesuits I met.' Now the question should be raised : Why did even we Shanghainese forget our own city's hero, Fr. Jacquinot?

Dr. Marcia Ristaino suggests that after World War II, China entered into a civil war, and then subsequent difficult times under Mao Zedong's leadership. As a historian born and educated in Shanghai, I have to add some concrete details to describe why we neglected Fr. Jacquinot's contribution. During the Cultural Revolution, all the activity associated with the Catholic church was a kind of trouble we needed to avoid. Fathers and nuns were looked upon by the cultural revolutionary ideology as "counter-revolutionaries". In 1996, when I worked in the Institute of History in SASS, I asked one of my senior colleagues who had compiled the Year Book of Modern Shanghai (*xiandai Shanghai dashiji*), why they collected just a few article about the Nanshi safety zone? Why had they only barely mentioned Rao Jiaju (饶家驹, Fr. Jacquinot's Chinese name), not even implying he was a Jesuit? He said that the times were difficult even in the 1980s.

These old stories recall to us the past decades we Shanghainese experienced. I don't think this kind of neglect came naturally, but from a class struggle. We Shanghainese really wanted to appreciate anyone who helped us during such a cruel period as during the Anti Japanese War, but the arguments between parties, nations, religions, and classes stopped us from expressing our thanks. That was the lesson we all needed. Because of this, when a diploma issued by Fr. Jacquinot to Xu Jia Hui refugee camp was found in a Macao antique shop last year, we Chinese were overjoyed to buy it without consideration of the price. This diploma now is displayed in the Tu San Wan Museum.

Now, my daughter who is a senior and an undergraduate student in the Department of History, Fudan University, just finished her thesis on the Jacquinot Safety Zone. She focused on Chinese materials and had the benefit of reading historian, Marcia Ristaino's book. It was a surprise that there are lot of contemporary reports in Shen Bao, Xinwen Bao, and other Chinese publications about the Rao Jiaju, and the Jacquinot Zone in Shanghai. I hope someone can take on the responsibility to translate Marcia Ristaino's book into Chinese. I believe, from now on, we Shanghainese cannot ever forget Fr. Jacquinot, and his contribution to the city.

Peking Sun, Shanghai Moon: A Chinese Memoir

Peking Sun, Shanghai Moon: a China Memoir by Diana Hutchins Angulo. Edited by Tess Johnston. Hong Kong: Old China Hand Press, 2008.

Reviewed by Janet Roberts

Like a contemporary Chinese scroll unfurling, this memoir by Diana Hutching Angulo, edited by Tess Johnston and Jean Anne A. Hauswald, provides scenarios in a series of quiet reflective moments in distant years. Savored hours of childhood memories in Beijing and youthful days in Shanghai are recollected in tranquillity.

Equal portions of the book are devoted to the two venues, Beijing and Shanghai. With the appearance of a rather "slight" book, only 142 pages in length, with 55 pages, devoted to family album pictures, the narrative still proves a satisfying read. The first third details life in Beijing, where the author's father was a military attaché, and the last third discusses a brief interlude in Hawaii, but mostly, life among the wealthy in Shanghai, in the 1930's-40's when the author's father was commander in chief of the Asian Fleet, – giving us snapshot views of people and occasions, and fashionable dinners.

Among the luminaries who appear in the pages in Beijing are friends of her parents, such as a Mr. Rogers who eventually gives Wallis Simpson away in marriage; visitors at their home, include Father Pierre Teilhard de Chardin; Roy Andrews and Sven Hedin; and notably, her mother's friend Princess Der Ling, as well as Reginald Johnson, tutor to Pu Yi . With a father who was a military envoy, diplomatic circles are dramatic backdrops for eliciting from the experience of a small girl, recall of scenes with elegant characters in a strictly ordered world. The memoir conveys these impressions, filtered through memory.

One of Diana Hutchins Angulo's more striking travel reminiscences, rests in showing how common warlord violence, pirating and banditry were in the days they ventured out on excursions from Beijing. In retrospect, the author comments on the "frightening warnings of terrorist activities that discourage many international travelers. I sometimes wonder at the courage of the many foreigners who made a home in China during this troubled period of history."

Diana Hutchins recalls a mosaic of personalities, in both sisters' lives, as well as life in the old French Concession in their home on 24 Ferguson Lane. Among the collage of a backdrop of clubs, balls, and parties in Shanghai – along with mention of her older sister's friendships – including anecdotes of Emily Hahn – Diana remembers a "vibrant girl, Agnes MacGruder...who met and married in Paris,... the well known Russian painter Ashile Gorky." Another young English girl, Peggy Hookham, who went to the same Cathedral School for Girls, trained with a former member of the Bolshoi in Shanghai, and became known to the world as Dame Margot Fonteyn.

In a short pastiche, the essays detail quotes of books read, stories heard, cultural understanding gained, childhood memories of her parents' friends, and her own school friends in Shanghai – the reflections of a woman in her 90th year, now living in Bryn Mawr, Pennsylvania, USA, near her daughter and grandsons. Having departed from China in 1940, she visited China, in this past decade, with a group of French journalists and artists, the highlight being a visit to her old home, No. 1 the Bund in Shanghai. Diana Hutchins writes the "greatest gift from my China days was one off the most precious that my parents could have given me: the ability to mingle with ease in an international community. In the years to come I was to live with confidence and pleasure on distant shores and in faraway places." The whole memoir is written with a sense of the light touch of a white gloved hand, leaving the reader with a sense of the author's quiet repose.

EAVESDROPPING ON A THREE-YEAR CONVERSATION
Missy's China: Letters from Hangzhou 1934-1937 by Doris Arnold, Ed. Tess Johnston. Hong Kong: Old China Hand Press, 2009.

REVIEWED BY LINDSAY SHEN

This collection of correspondence imparts the pleasures of overhearing one side of a conversation that took place—sometimes daily—in the tumultuous years leading up to the Sino-Japanese War. Between June 1934 when Doris Arnold and her two sons left the United States, until May 1937 when they departed Hangzhou, Arnold wrote detailed letters about her life in China to her mother and sister in Ilion, New York. The diligence of her communication has resulted in a volume of some 500 pages of rich description of expatriate life in 1930s Hangzhou.

On the surface, though, the circumstances of the Arnolds' China sojourn may seem to merit a digest, rather than unabridged publication (the editor indicates that she eliminated none of the Hangzhou letters.) George Arnold, Doris' husband, was an American engineer who was on an assignment with an aircraft factory. Doris' own life revolved almost entirely around her household and especially her two sons. Apart from some part-time teaching and volunteering, she had no profession that allowed her to interface with the Chinese community or gain any special experience of Chinese culture or business. And, as she herself stressed to her family, she was writing from the provincial city of Hangzhou—not the glamorous and cosmopolitan Shanghai. Social and cultural life was restricted, and contact with Chinese limited to servants plus an intriguing couple who became close family friends, Colonel and Mrs. Wong. The deteriorating political situation in eastern China is rarely mentioned.

However, the value of this book—in its bulky entirety—lies in part in its ordinariness; this is the sort of raw material on which social history depends. *Missy's China* is not a volume that purports to shed any special light on Chinese culture or society, but it does portray, on an intimate, quotidian level, and from a woman's perspective, the efforts of an expatriate family to acclimatize to life in a Chinese city. These letters relate valiant (often doomed) efforts to conduct a life similar in its comforts to the life they had left behind. Locating palatable food, suitable clothing, agreeable companionship, stimulating recreation—this is the bread and butter of this correspondence. Despite the banality of some of the subject matter, Arnold is always engaging, and sometimes highly humourous—for example in her descriptions of the tensions between those in China on business assignments, and the missionary families with whom they were often uneasy bedfellows: "We have had continuous rain since my last letter to you and it's most depressing, disheartening and a lot of other "d's" not very becoming in a missionary neighborhood." (p.353)

It is in her observations of her children, though, that Arnold is often most poignant. Expatriate childhood is an under-researched topic, and one that *Missy's China* helps illuminate. While writers such as J.G. Ballard and Pearl Buck have recollected aspects of their childhoods in China, these are, by nature, distorted by temporal distance. The experiences of the Arnolds' two sons are of course mediated by their mother, and edited for transmission to their American family, but they are nonetheless valuable as "real-time" observations. Over the course of three years we learn much about the loneliness of children, and their efforts to create their own space and identities in a culture that was sometimes indulgent, sometimes openly hostile: "It doesn't hurt to be called 'foreign devils' but it's not so nice to have dirty people grab at you, spit at you, pull off the children's hats, snap dirty towels at you and throw sugar cane etc. to hit you. Scott doesn't seem to mind, but if I were small it would give me nightmares." (p. 255) There are of course many pleasures: picnics, boat trips, and the construction of "the whale" – a swimming pool rigged from a factory crate. However life was rather precarious for small children, and Arnold writes with great sensitivity and empathy about the many illnesses suffered by her own children and those of her friends.

It is easy to become absorbed in these letters—to become anxious, for example, over the fate of a child suffering from scarlet fever, or hospitalized for a mysterious paralysis. And possibly because of the personal qualities of the "protagonists," we wish we knew a little more about them. While the editorial aim was to allow "the voice to be entirely Missy's," the lack of background information on Arnold's life can mean that these letters are disorientating for the reader, especially at the beginning; the half-page foreword does little to situate us, to tell us what business brought the family to China, or what ages the children were. A biographical preface could have solved mysteries that the reader is left guessing at until well into the text.

However, Arnold's commentary is so valuable that we

are willing to follow along, put aside puzzles over identities, and feel gratitude that a small private press can make heard a voice that might otherwise be left silent.

A STUDY OF THE NORTH CHINA BRANCH OF THE ROYAL ASIATIC SOCIETY BY WANG YI

Shanghai: Shanghai Book House Press, 2005.

REVIEWED BY DR. LIU WEI AND DR. JUDITH KOLBAS

Wang Yi's study of the history of the North China Branch of the Royal Asiatic Society was originally a Ph.D. thesis for Fudan University in Shanghai. It is an excellent account in Chinese of the entire 97 years of the North China Branch from 1857 to 1954. The author's main source is the *Journal* of the NCB (*JNCBRAS*), of which the Fudan University Library possesses the only surviving complete set. Dr. Wang also consulted most other English and Japanese learned journals, such as the *Numismatic and Philatelic Journal of Japan*, and newspapers published in China during the period.

The author pictures the NCB as the single most important institution for introducing matters Chinese to the wider world for a whole century and the lynchpin of Chinese-based Sinology. He concludes that 'Its contribution to intellectual communication far exceeded its service to colonialism.' His analysis of the nature of research work carried out by different foreign nationals is also insightful. Indeed, the many renowned scholars included Sven Hedin, Col. Nikolai Prejewalsky, Oswald Siren, Paul Pelliot as well as a host of British experts such as W.S. Basil, who contributed an article on 'The Hsi-Hsia Dynasty or the Tangut', and Bernard E. Read on 'The Dragon in Chinese Medicine' to the *Journal*. Besides scholars, barons and Chinese princes rubbed shoulders with missionaries and the military like the young Lt.-Col Gordon later of Sudan fame. Moreover, many libraries were members of the Society, including the ones of Stanford University, the Essex Institute, the University of Shanghai, the University of Rangoon, the South Manchurian Railway, the American

Women's Club, the Hangzhou Christian College, the India Office, Beijing University, the Institute of Chinese Cultural Studies, Mysore University and the Frankfurt China Institute. The Society published four catalogues of the library, the last in 1909; and its museum became the foundation for the now world-famous Shanghai Museum on People's Square, initiating the concept in China of public access to displays of scientific discoveries and to collections of the country's cultural heritage.

One of the book's primary merits is the compilation of statistics and the organisation of the chronological development of the North China Branch. Dr. Wang expended considerable effort in tracking down the names and occupations of the 3,000 plus total number of members over the years (appendix 2), the presidents and their terms as well as over 700 lectures with their speakers and topics (appendix 1). He has listed these and other reference details with great clarity in the text and in extensive appendices.

Since the author's focus is on the activities of the North China Branch, he provides only a brief mention on page 27 in ten lines of its demise, which occurred from 1952 to 1955 because of Communist control, and the handover of its assets to the Shanghai municipal government. It is, therefore, incumbent on others perhaps to determine the current whereabouts and present status of the 94,000 volumes the Society held at the time of the takeover and of the museum collections. In addition, he has chosen to mention, again only briefly, the Royal Asiatic Society building: it was constructed in 1932, and the cover of his book has a clear and precise but somewhat nostalgic line sketch of the façade. Nevertheless in 1999, the Shanghai municipal government listed the building at 20 Huqui Road, just behind the Bund near the Peace Hotel, as an architectural heritage site, which in 2006 has a plaque to that effect and is being restored. The building was designed by the Hong Kong firm of Palmer and Turner, which had constructed the HSBC headquarters in Hong Kong in the 1920s, the most expensive building in Hong Kong to that date. The firm was also the best known and most active one in Shanghai in the same period. It would seem, consequently, that there is ample material and interest for Dr. Wang to continue his project.

For all those interested in the intellectual history of modern China and the creation of Chinese studies worldwide, which were intimately associated with the Royal Asiatic Society, this study is an essential reference. It is also a welcome harbinger of the slow but steady intellectual rigour that scholarship is developing in China.

Editorial Note: This review was originally published in the *Journal of the Royal Asiatic Society* (Third Series), Volume 17:1, January 2007. The NCBRAS library now belongs to the Shanghai Library, and may be consulted at the Xujiahui Biblioteca.

CONTRIBUTORS

FRIEDERIKE ASSANDRI is Research Associate, University of Heidelberg.
CHEN ZU'EN is Professor of Modern Chinese History at Donghua University.
NENAD DJORDJEVIC is former consul-gerant of the Serbian Consulate-General in Shanghai.
PAUL FRENCH is a Shanghai-based writer and historian.
PETER HIBBARD is a Shanghai-based historian and President of the Royal Asiatic Society China in Shanghai.
TESS JOHNSTON is a Shanghai-based writer, researcher and lecturer.
JUDITH KOLBAS revived the Royal Asiatic Society in China, in Hangzhou in 2006.
LI TIANGANG is Professor of Religion, Fudan University, Shanghai.
ANDREA LINGENFELTER is a poet and translator of Chinese literature.
LIU WEI is Professor of History and Politics, Zhejiang University.
THOMAS MCCARTHY is an Irish poet, novelist and critic.
JAMES MILLER is Associate Professor of Chinese Religions at Queen's University, Ontario, Canada.
JANET ROBERTS is a writer, professor of English and Women's Studies at SISU, and Honorary Editor of the Royal Asiatic Society China in Shanghai.
LINDSAY SHEN is Principal Lecturer, Sino British College, and Honorary Editor, Royal Asiatic Society China in Shanghai.
KIM TAYLOR is founder of Kaimu Productions, a Shanghai-based documentary film production company, and Honorary Librarian, Royal Asiatic Society China in Shanghai.
EMILY DE WOLF PETTIT is a consultant, and Director of an independent China-based arts consultancy.
ZHANG JIANGUO is Director of the Weihai Archives Bureau.
ZHANG JUNYONG is Director, Editorial and Research Department, Weihai Archives Bureau.

www.ingramcontent.com/pod-product-compliance
Lightning Source LLC
LaVergne TN
LVHW012017060526
838201LV00061B/4353